Limitless

Limitless

Ajaz Ahmed

Vermilion
LONDON

5 7 9 10 8 6

Vermilion, an imprint of Ebury Publishing,
20 Vauxhall Bridge Road,
London SW1V 2SA

Vermilion is part of the Penguin Random Home group of companies
whose addresses can be found at global.penguinrandomhome.com

Penguin
Random House
UK

First published by Vermilion in 2015

www.eburypublishing.co.uk

A CIP catalogue record for this book is available from
the British Library

Hardback ISBN 9780091955045
Paperback ISBN 9780091955434

Printed and bound in Great Britain by Clays Ltd, St Ives PLC

To my father Khowaj and my mother Sughran, who gave me a limitless love of learning and liberty.

Contents

'In three words I can sum up everything
I've learned about life: it goes on.'

Robert Frost

'Study the past if you would define
the future'

Confucius

Introduction:

The business of business

BEFORE IT WAS an interest group or an academic discipline, business was what happened when people came together to offer things they had in exchange for things they wanted or needed.

While we can trace the origins of the modern institutions and conventions of business to particular times and places, its primal essence goes back far beyond recorded history – back to the origins of human society itself. Business came before the idea of money, or the idea of the nation state. Business, in its best and broadest sense, isn't something you can be 'pro' or 'anti', because it is as basic and vital a part of civilisation as language, or marriage or ritual.

The English word 'business' originally just meant being active and engaged. It was doing something that kept you *busy* – in the good sense, not in a mindless 'busywork' way. 'Business' was what the craftsperson did when a commission came in; it was how the farmer harvested enough crops to exchange with a neighbour or a neighbouring village, thereby ensuring his family survived the winter. Business was the adventurous spirit of the ancient peoples who set out in boats to trade shells and spices for the fruits of foreign lands. It's the very same appetite for adventure – for enthusiastically embarking into the unknown in search of new commodities and new customers – that has distinguished determined leaders and their businesses ever since.

crisis and challenge are encoded into the basic formula of every compelling story. That's why the lessons we absorb from a story of great leadership linger with us in ways dates and statistics alone can't.

But the more we have professionalised and theorised about the business of business, the easier we have made it for ourselves to forget these fundamental truths. Since the dawn of capitalism and the advent of the industrial age, we've been able to access evermore information, speculation and analysis about what 'business' is.

In the past decade, digital technology has multiplied the volume of data and expert discussion we can access beyond all previous imagining. This new information can be massively useful – but only as long as it doesn't prevent us from being able to draw back and see the bigger picture. Trying to keep up with all the trappings of modern business can sometimes distract our attention from the handful of simple, timeless truths that exist about doing it well.

No limits

THERE ARE FIVE principles to which I believe outstanding businesses – of whatever size, era or market segment – unfailingly return. Considered collectively, these strengths – the impulses to *Democratise*, *Revolutionise*, *Simplify*, *Organise* and *Author* – are all defined by a quality I call Limitless. These principles endure precisely because they are not strict instructions about what and what not to do. Instead they are injunctions to keep thinking about how your organisation relates to the people within it and the world beyond it. They are reminders never to rest on fossilised dogmas, never to unquestionably assent to the assumptions of today. That way, you can see the opportunities and interconnections others might be too blinkered to imagine.

Akio Morita knew the feudal Japan he was born into was headed for change after World War II, despite the propaganda efforts of the government. His foresight was crucial to the half-century of unrivalled success enjoyed by Sony, the company he founded. Coco Chanel eschewed the constraints of the corset, the restrictions of fussy fabrics, the mannequin mentality and seasonal gimmickry of the fashion establishment to make clothes that fit women's lives – rather than the other way – and thereby forged an idea like no other. Henry Ford and Thomas Edison were the tycoons of the industrial age that helped establish America as a nation of full economic participation, making it the richest, most inventive and most productive country on earth. Bill Gates and Steve Jobs, the giants of the digital age, continued this tradition. Gates made his fortune in technology and now presides over the world's largest private philanthropic enterprise, deploying its vast resources to enhance healthcare and reduce extreme poverty around the world, while also expanding educational opportunities and access to information technology in America. Jobs returned to a disenchanted Apple, catapulting it back into prosperity, while revolutionising several industries and creating history's most valuable company. At Netflix, Reed Hastings did away with spurious rules and regulations and outflanked better-resourced rivals to establish a fast-moving entertainment brand that soon set the pace for the entire industry.

Risk was inherent and acknowledged in all these ventures, but risk is inherent (and too often ignored) in any business – *especially* those that doggedly stand still as the world around them changes. When our Limitless heroes faced and embraced the reality of risk, the returns were dizzying. Many of them failed before they succeeded, but, as we will see in the stories that follow, crisis and challenge are encoded into the basic formula of every compelling story. That's why the lessons we absorb from a story of great leadership linger with us in ways dates and statistics alone can't.

It wasn't blind egotism that gave these leaders the assurance to ignore received wisdom and established assumptions about how things had to be done. Their confidence came from their faith in people and in the power of good ideas. They didn't try to impose rigid thinking on a changing world, but responded to change around them with boundless generosity, optimism and endeavour. The notion of business as a kind of conquest ignores the fact that enduring leadership is about service to your public, not giving them orders. Understood in that context, the pursuit of profit isn't the be-all and end-all; it's the indicator that makes you rethink your approach if your public declines to vote with its wallets.

every great company is great because of the way it responds to the one-off context in which it exists.

In many respects, the things that really count are the things we still can't reduce to accountancy and enumeration. Rather than being a formula about investment and return or profit and loss, being Limitless is about having an expansive outlook on the world. It's a broad-minded capacity to perceive possibilities beyond those imaginable in your immediate context. Rather than allowing people to cling to the seeming safety of prejudices and presumptions, it obliges them to face the future in a positive and energised way.

Influential leaders in modern business history never let themselves forget this underlying truth. For all their varied experiences, approaches and achievements, the heroes featured in this book never lost sight of the simple qualities that define a better business. That's why they nurtured organisations and ideas that outlasted all comers. That's why their examples remain peerless repositories of knowledge, inspiration and wisdom.

people crave 'proven' formulas for business success because they want to be indemnified against the possibility of failure and relieved of the burden of thinking for themselves. Smart leaders circumvent this compulsion by reformulating wisdom and insights to inspire new thoughts, rather than slavishly copying pre-existing solutions.

In their different ways, these trailblazers channelled the core principles of good business better than the rest. They reached out to more people than their rivals. They changed the world because they had visions they knew how to share with the rest of us. They looked upon corporate organisation not as an obligation, but an opportunity. They didn't allow their own cleverness to distract them from the virtues of simplicity.

AGED 21, I helped to found AKQA. As an all-digital start-up, AKQA embodied everything that's most celebrated in the entrepreneurial aspirations of today. Since then, we've gone from start-up to an enterprise with over 2,000 employees across 17 offices around the world. The journey – always educational and often difficult – makes it clear that staying true to our founding ethos is a constant, but immensely satisfying challenge.

In the face of the inevitable growing pains and problems, I found myself turning away from the business quarterlies and the daily news feeds to the tales of the influences, leaders and organisations that inspired me at a time before AKQA and continue to provide perpetual motivation to the present day.

the best leaders have the courage and empathy to help their colleagues, customers and community lead better lives.

The way those legends created companies that survived global upheaval and generational change provided perspective and enlightenment. They provided examples of staying lean and responsive as a business grows and inevitably becomes more elaborate. They offered boundless proof of the merit of having a conversation with as many people as you could, and, time and time again, they demonstrated that the best way to bring about change is to give your all to the present so the public is able to benefit fully from the future you envision.

business isn't something we do; it's everything we are.

Fascinating, uplifting and complex, those pioneers gave us unforgettable quotations, stirring speeches and inspirational ideas, but not instruction manuals. They didn't presume to leave behind how-to guides for future leaders. They knew that every great company is great because of the way it responds to the one-off context in which it exists. They knew that you couldn't cut and paste a bulletproof business plan or management style guide from another place and time and hope to succeed in yours, because no two situations or environments are the same.

The legacy the pioneers do leave to those hoping to learn from them – the one that unites all their varied achievements – is spectacular market proof of the value of an open, enquiring mind. There's a reason why it's called leadership: the moments in which you really earn the name are the ones for which there is no handbook. The moments in which every possible choice is tough and fraught with risk are the ones that make or break you. It's when life is thrown out of balance – when you face tough competition or the economy is thrown suddenly into recession – these moments of crisis, and the required resilience with which you react to them, become the defining events that shape destinies.

People crave 'proven' formulas for business success because they want to be indemnified against of the possibility of failure and relieved of the burden of thinking for themselves. Smart leaders circumvent this compulsion by reformulating wisdom and insights to inspire new thoughts, rather than slavishly copying pre-existing solutions.

The reason a Limitless outlook has endured through numerous generations of belief systems, commercial markets and leaps in scientific understanding is that its adherents have all rejected the unchallenged cultural assumptions of their day. Instead, they heeded their own direct perception and strived to examine the life of things below the surface. They gained their edge not through cynicism or mercenary moves but by being more open to

it is through stories, not numbers, that human beings make sense of the world. Stories are what survive of human culture. And the ones that endure do so because each generation is able to find new perspectives and lessons in them. They discover ways to adapt and adopt ancient truths into modern reality.

possibility than their peers, by being alert to everything around them and by prizing possibility and promise over established limits and the status quo.

if we can get a better perspective on our present by learning from the wisdom of the past, we might also catch a glimpse of a whole new Limitless future.

Good leaders don't inflict their fears and insecurities on others and then rationalise them to make themselves feel better. The best leaders have the courage and empathy to help their colleagues, customers and community lead better lives. They see the humanity in others and therefore deal with people and situations in a compassionate way.

Limitless leaders have a sense of 'enoughness' in their personal lives. They focus their energy on making an unlimited contribution to the world's progress and preservation. They know of the dangers of inequity. They are aware of the limitations of our planet and that the inexhaustible plundering of the earth's precious irreplaceable resources, if left unchecked, will create environmental catastrophes of the kind that there is no 'undo' button. Today's most progressive leaders understand that the only growth that is healthy and sustainable is the growth of quality across everything an organisation does.

In *Limitless*, I've gathered the stories and insights of leadership that have meant the most to me. Most of them are true tales of individuals who founded and sustained world-beating businesses, but I've also included ideas from the philosophies of the *shokunin* and the mandala.

These ideas celebrated in *Limitless* are not explicit rules you can learn by heart and apply without thinking – if they were, they would have already gone wrong and rusty. Statistics and rigid strategies can become meaningless with the passage of time. It is through stories, not numbers, that human beings make sense of the world. Stories are what survive of human culture. And the ones that endure do so because each generation is able to find new perspectives and lessons in them. They discover ways to adapt and adopt ancient truths into modern reality.

The five timeless principles endure precisely because – like stories – they aren't strict instructions about what and what not to do. Instead, they are imperatives to keep thinking about how your company relates to the people within it and the world outside it. They are reminders to remain open to a progressive future instead of restricting your thoughts according to the established boundaries of today.

The supreme value of story to convey the potential of business has never really been in doubt. I believe that the tales of hundred-year-old companies might contain more wisdom than the newest management fads and their simplistic explanations of success. The true stories of triumph, tribulation, trial and error behind big firms may well provide a better grounding for the day-to-day reality of doing business. Stories that resonate are about human nature, which is why they stand the test of time.

Business isn't something we do; it's everything we are. If we choose to embrace that fact rather than bury our heads, the scope we have is without bounds.

Fear eats the soul, but hope nourishes it. Optimism is essential if you're going to break through accepted barriers. If we can get a better perspective on our present by learning from the wisdom of the past, we might also catch a glimpse of a whole new Limitless future.

Five Principles *of* Leadership
that Endures

Democratise

LIMITLESS LEADERS ARE never the type to settle for being big fish in small ponds. With egalitarian vision and aiming to make a sustained contribution, they give themselves the greatest chance of creating real change by giving to the many what is held by the few.

Revolutionise

THE MOST TRANSFORMATIVE organisations and teams aren't the ones whose leaders shout the loudest. To oversee a business revolution, you don't just need a compelling vision of the future; you also require the quiet perceptiveness, adaptability and human awareness to make it a living reality.

Simplify

TO BENEFIT THE most from an ethos of simplicity, you must have a sincere personal belief in its virtues. Limitless leaders believe that the simple will always displace the complex. To make your mark in a world overloaded with complexity and information, you need a clear, concise voice and the fewest steps possible between your idea and its fulfilment.

Organise

CONVENTIONAL WISDOM HOLDS that efficiency and creativity are rival forces, but in truth they're better handled as two parts of a single dynamic. Relentlessly improving and evolving systems will deliver a continuous stream of excellence as organisations adapt, expand, get resilient and grow. Think of it as superior output through constant adaptation.

Author

EVERYTHING AN ORGANISATION does is part of a narrative, because every aspect of human understanding is shaped by story. If you want to lead your organisation to exceptional feats, you have to embrace and assert your own story, and the responsibilities of authorship.

Democratise

Exclusivity for everyone.

If you want it, why

shouldn't everybody else?

for Optimum Impact,
Maximise Reach

IN TIMES ANALOGUE and digital, ancient and modern, richer and poorer, one rudimentary formula has stood Limitless businesses in good stead: the wider the audience you can connect with, the more relevant your organisation is, and the greater your chances of building something that lasts.

It's a vision of egalitarianism that legendary entrepreneurs have embraced. The fact is that many achieve the most impact by daring to believe they know what other people want simply because, as consumers, they want it too. Richard Branson, for example, has often attributed his motivation for starting his air travel and telecommunications businesses to his personal frustration at suffering the services of what were effectively national monopolies.

He's far from the only entrepreneur to have founded enduring organisations by setting himself alongside, rather than apart from, the people; to have focused on basic human qualities and customer service in areas where, thanks to market domination and complacent corporate cultures, those things have been forgotten.

the fact is that many achieve the most impact by daring to believe they know what other people want simply because, as consumers, they want it too.

A striking number of Limitless businesses began when an entrepreneur tried something new, and liked it enough to put their faith in the idea that others would like it too. That variously meant i) inventing something new, ii) making an existing product or service better or more widely available and affordable, or iii) seeing a great idea in one territory and then taking it to another. One way or another, the bravest and truest entrepreneurs have almost always been about the extension of access.

Before the business plans, the bank loans and the big time, most of the heroes of this chapter had a long-cherished feeling that other people would love the same things they did. For Henry Ford, it was the horseless carriage, also known as 'the automobile'. For Margaret Rudkin, it meant baking more of the bread she'd originally devised for her sickly son. For Dietrich Mateschitz, it was an exotic Asian product category that, thanks to his efforts, we all now know as the 'energy drink'. In the case of Bill Gates, the driver was less personal taste and more a passionate conviction that as many people as possible should have access to a basic necessity of modern life; in his time in business that meant software, and once he became a philanthropist that meant vaccines. If the urge to democratise new things by making them more readily available were not such a driver for businesses, our world would look staggeringly different today.

Because these great democratising entrepreneurs loved the things they'd discovered, they were able to withstand the doubters early on – there were plenty such doubters, and there always will be when untested ideas surface.

When you're trying something new because you think it's great, and nobody else seems to get it, a deeply held, passionate belief that other people, lots of people, *will* get it – one day – is an incomparable asset. It not only gives you strength and solace when you want to throw in the towel but it also obliges you to keep refining your offering and the way you communicate it until you make that big breakthrough.

Today, winning ideas take off and can leap across continents in seconds but it was always true that if just one person knew they were on to something good, the masses would come round eventually. The process may have dramatically accelerated in our digital world, but that doesn't mean tomorrow's leaders don't have plenty to learn from the democratisers who did it first.

one way or another, the bravest and truest entrepreneurs have almost always been about the extension of access.

Henry Ford:

For the Great Multitude

WHEN HENRY FORD first asked for a vote to endorse the most influential decision he would ever make, he consulted a constituency of one. Though the loyalty of the masses would be central to his future success, in 1899 Ford wanted to know how his immediate plans would impact upon the person who had most to lose from them: his wife, Clara.

As he told her, it was 'make or break' time for his dream. He was 36, and the couple had a young child, Edsel, to think about. But Henry needed Clara to believe in him, and in the potential of his big idea, because he wanted to ditch his secure, prestigious $125-a-month job to try to turn the dream into a reality. People had been talking about the concept of the 'horseless carriage' since the invention of the steam engine, but to most 'experts' and industrialists, it was as outrageous a pipe dream as the concept of the 'driverless car' was to most of us way back in 2010.

Ford had first encountered a gasoline-driven farm engine in his early twenties. After that initial revelation, he painstakingly researched scientific journals on the subject, going on to build his own experimental internal-combustion engines and simple 'gasoline buggies' powered by them. He scared the horses and annoyed the pedestrians in his native Detroit with all his engine noise, but in doing so he was also able to drive 1,000 miles in the second buggy he'd built to a new, improved design, before he sold it to a wealthy enthusiast for $2,000. He travelled to New York and visited Macy's to see the first arrival on American shores of the latest model from a German company called Benz, but Ford was unimpressed by the expensive imported automobile's weight and complex design, and remained confident that his own research had already eclipsed it.

Ford's after-hours experiments never stopped, and reports of them had impressed colleagues at the Edison Illuminating Company, where he had been promoted to chief engineer by the mid-1890s. Inevitably, his talent ensured that he soon got to meet the company's legendary founder. Thomas Edison was impressed by Ford's experiments with gasoline engines but saw them as merely a 'charming hobby'. Perhaps understandably, the great inventor was too fixed on his grand plans for electricity – by no means a passing foible – to endorse such a potential distraction for a senior employee. Prototyping something as novel as a gasoline-powered carriage was going to be no small task. Edison countered by offering Ford a promotion to a role that would effectively make him his right-hand man. But the impressive offer came with the caveat that the younger man must commit to ending his investigations with internal-combustion engines.

History came close to witnessing what might have been the first industrial 'dream team'. But in the end, a Ford–Edison partnership was not to be. In August 1899, with Clara's crucial vote of confidence, Henry Ford left Edison's company and immediately attracted partners and financial speculators, all of whom loved his pitch, and he entered the automobile business.

in terms of what made a viable business, Ford saw that there were no eternal rules. Change was the only constant.

However, as is often the case, 'He who pays the piper calls the tune.' Ford's investors appointed him to the position of chief engineer but, with just a small shareholding in the start-up company, he soon became frustrated by his powerlessness. Like Steve Jobs many years later, he wanted the product to be the idea around which the business was engineered, but his investors made decisions strictly on the basis of how much they could make on a sale, and by responding to the moves of their rivals. Ford was horrified at this utterly unimaginative approach because he believed the only thing it guaranteed was long-term failure. At the time, he wrote:

The essence of my idea then is that waste and greed block the delivery of true service. Both waste and greed are unnecessary. Waste is due largely to not understanding what one does, or being careless in doing of it. Greed is merely a species of nearsightedness.

An affordable Ford

SURE ENOUGH THAT first car company soon failed, and by the beginning of 1901, Ford had decided he needed to start again – but this time he'd be doing things *his* way. He spent the next couple of years working in and around the nascent automobile industry, building his expertise and the profile of his name. The Ford Motor Company was formally established in 1903. That marked the birth of a business legend, and the roots of a philosophy that would soon produce the car in which half of America would learn to drive; the car that, exactly 100 years after Ford left Edison's employ, was voted 'Car of the Century' by a jury of 126 experts from the Global Automotive Elections Foundation: the iconic Model T.

Henry Ford is justly remembered for that car, and not simply because of its pivotal role in establishing the automobile as an accessible everyday item. Beyond any one product, he is celebrated as the father of 'Fordism' – the term given to the way his mass-production manufacturing techniques changed consumer expectations and working conditions that sparked what was tantamount to a second industrial revolution. At its core, Fordism provided a template for successful twentieth-century industrial production that would endure for decades.

But Ford was not merely a master engineer. His practical achievements were products of his broader, people-focused philosophy. That's why his greatest insights are for the ages, and not just for the bygone golden age of the motorcar. He inadvertently helped create the market for one of the twentieth century's key commodities – oil. Paradoxically, Ford also openly praised the nineteenth-century biofuel pioneers he'd seen burn surplus corn to power their farms. He looked forward to a future when people wouldn't have to plunder the earth's finite resources to power their machines. Henry Ford intuitively knew that some unforeseen change would change the transport landscape even more significantly than the Model T.

In terms of what made a viable business, Ford saw that there were no eternal rules. Change was the only constant. As he wrote in *My Life and Work*:

> If to petrify is success, all one has to do is humour the lazy side of the mind, but if to grow is success, then one must wake up anew every morning and keep awake all day. I saw great businesses become but the ghost of a name because someone thought they could be managed just as they were always managed, and though the management may have been most excellent in its day, its excellence consisted in its alertness to its day, and not in slavish following of its yesterdays.

HOWEVER, FORD'S OWN philosophy and the media face of 'Fordism' diverged. In his time, Ford and his pared-down approach to product design were praised as the shining example of twentieth-century organisation.

'Standardisation' – whereby simplicity of design and scale of production were combined to create an efficient, economical product – was the key. But Ford usually took the word as an insult: he would frequently point out that his 'standardised' process was actually one that was constantly changing thanks to new technologies and practices. (Toyota, today the world's largest car manufacturer, is famed for its continuous improvement philosophy, known as *kaizen* – Japanese for 'good change'.)

Furthermore, Ford felt you could only truly serve the masses if you gave them tools they could use in numerous situations; that any great product must, by definition, be endlessly adaptable, rather than uniform and inflexible. That was why he would often proudly tell the story of one particular Model T engine that spent 15 years on the road under various owners, before being removed from the car to see out its days as a powerful pump which, with the aid of a mule, drew water from the well on a farm in New Mexico.

Ford regarded his cars not so much as standardised but as simple enough to be easy to drive, understand and repair. A Model T would fit the unique lives and needs of millions of very different people precisely because it was such a utilitarian design.

There was another reason Henry Ford insisted on re-defining 'standardisation' before he was willing to take credit for inventing the concept: he felt it implied a rigidity of approach, a set and inflexible way of doing things that would soon fracture and shatter when change came round the corner.

'There is', Ford wrote, 'a subtle danger in the man thinking that he is "fixed" for life. It indicates that the next jolt of progress is going to fling him off.' Like Heraclitus – the Stoic philosopher, famed for his pronouncement that 'No man ever steps into the same river twice, for it's not the same river and he's not the same man' – Ford believed everything was always in motion. He was committed to no fixed principle, design or energy source for eternity. At his best, Ford's drive to democratise drove him to embrace whatever changes came his way. That was the secret of his philosophy – the spiritual Tao of Henry Ford that lay behind the material success of his company's most success-ful products. As he wrote:

> Life, as I see it, is not a location but a journey ... Everything is in flux, and was meant to be. Life flows. We may live at the same number of the street, but it is never the same man who lives there.

Like so many of the heroes of this book, Ford's innate sense of a cosmos in constant change gave him a massive practical advantage. It ensured humility and openness to new ideas – ideas that he was able to convert into practical endeavour and what he called 'fair profit'. It meant that he genuinely believed it when he declared, 'Everything can always be done better than it is being done.' In line with this philosophy, he refreshingly insisted that nobody should ever describe themselves as 'an expert' simply on the basis that they knew their job well. To Ford, even describing something as 'impossible' was a sign of a closed mind and equivalent to surrender and defeat:

> I refuse to accept that there are impossibilities. I cannot discover that anyone knows enough about anything on this earth definitely to say what is and what is not possible.

In a universe of flux and flow, where most of the limits people lived within were falsely imposed upon themselves, and human knowledge was finite, an egalitarian business outlook was Ford's anchor. It was the reason that he could back an untried product with absolute assurance.

Ford's one unqualified conviction about commerce was that if you can deliver the best product to the most people at the best price, you will have the best chance of success. At the broadest level, this idea was not just a sales strategy, but the practical application of Ford's most deeply held convictions about the world. If fair products were made to serve the masses at prices they could afford, those people could thrive, enjoy their lives and feel rewarded for their labour.

An ardent pacifist, Ford saw war as the epitome of waste and greed. Despite sticking to his pro-peace, internationalist principles in a fervently patriotic climate, Ford ran for the US senate in 1918 at the request of President Woodrow Wilson and lost narrowly.

any great product must, by definition, be endlessly adaptable, rather than uniform and inflexible.

Almost a century later, in *The Better Angels of our Nature*, Harvard psychology professor and bestselling author Steven Pinker would cite commerce, and the social benefits and interactions it brings, as one of the key reasons human societies have become exponentially less violent. He asserted that commerce was one of five 'changes in our cultural and material milieu that have given our peaceable motives the upper hand.'

Like other Limitless leaders, Ford's sometimes mystical-sounding philosophy was one of these intuited truths that science and management schools would much later demonstrate with hard data and academic theses.

Ahead of his time

FORD'S WISDOM ANTICIPATED some of the most celebrated ideas of later business leaders too. Like Akio Morita, founder of Sony, Ford banned talk of past schools and prior jobs. Once somebody had been employed, Ford wanted to create a harmonious meritocracy based on present-day effectiveness and progress, not social class or nostalgia for a shared academic past. Like Netflix founder Reed Hastings, he paid employees over the market rate and shouted about it. In January 1914, Ford famously introduced a minimum daily wage of $5 – more than double the market average for factory work – and reduced the working day from nine to eight hours, believing better recruits who felt well rewarded would ultimately help the bottom line. (An idea statistically borne out by a 2013 McKinsey report on wages and productivity.) The business logic of Ford's idea of a virtuous circle of fair profit and fair reward was most gratifyingly validated when his factory workers bought Model Ts in droves. In 1914, a Ford production-line worker could buy a Model T with the equivalent of four months' Ford wages – not an equation that works at today's average car prices and pay scales.

Henry Ford was obsessed with minimising rules and hierarchies. Titles were bad for business, he believed, because they were a way for individuals to divide, rule and play power games, instead of coming together to help the whole company flourish. 'The division of responsibility according to titles', he argued, 'goes so far as to amount to a removal altogether of responsibility.'

In the 1920s, Ford commissioned 'an assessment', which found that almost half of the 8,000 jobs at his Detroit facilities could be done by people with disabilities, and so he promptly adjusted the company's recruiting policy to ensure their employment. He also didn't apologise when able-bodied workers found their roles replaced by new machinery; as he was fond of observing, it was automation and technical advancement that had drastically reduced the number of dangerous and unpleasant manual jobs in his factories. And, provided the company remained healthy, any employees displaced by new machines would naturally be found more fulfilling new jobs in emerging areas of the business.

A sense of reciprocal responsibility underpinned Ford's entire project and his understanding of the value of work itself. For Ford, as with so many leaders after him, one of the worst phrases an employee could utter was 'That's not my job'.

Taking it to the street

FROM DAY ONE, a 'can-do' culture was fundamental to Ford's success. When he first came on the scene there was no proven mass 'demand' for cars – just as a century later there was no pre-existing market for the iPad until Apple went out and created it. Since Ford was certain that the automobile was a highly practical product that would have wide appeal, it followed that his job was to design, manufacture, price and promote cars efficiently and effectively.

Sure enough, Ford's exponential sales increases came when, a few years into the Ford Motor Company's life, he pared down its product range to two models and refined their manufacture until each could be sold for half the price of other automobiles, even though they usually boasted superior reliability.

Henry Ford's vision of the versatility of the automobile was uncompromising, but he wasn't above bowing to popular taste in order to bring that vision to the people – even when doing so offended his own personal sensibilities. So, for example, in the company's early years, even though he didn't really approve of it, Ford oversaw a successful involvement in motor racing. Ford was highly frustrated by the fact that the media only saw cars as newsworthy when they raced, but he resigned himself to embracing that reality in pursuit of his greater goals. Accordingly, he applied his talents to engineering and driving great cars that won races and duly got his name and brand on the front pages.

rather than targeting a narrow demographic, start with the broadest possible ambition, and you stand the best chance of having the greatest cultural impact.

Having used racing to get his name in the public eye, though, Ford made sure his advertising copy went against convention by emphasising the versatility and practicality of his cars. Ford didn't want to package the car as some symbol of sex appeal. Instead, once his name was widely known, he became committed to promotion as a means of explaining the wide utilitarian uses to which cars would be put by ordinary people: Ford ads of the day featured family picnics and shopping trips, rather than focusing on power and speed.

Patently outrageous

THIS PEOPLE-FOCUSED PHILOSOPHY helped the company endure the inevitable challenges of being a start-up, and also allowed Ford to outdo the aggressive attempts of rivals to put the new company out of business. Unbeknown to Ford and many other automotive entrepreneurs (including Karl Benz, who filed his own patent some years later), a patent for a 'safe, cheap and simple *road locomotive*' had been filed in 1879 by one George Baldwin Seldon, an inventor and patent lawyer from Rochester, New York.

Seldon's patent contained no meaningful technical detail, but read more like a wish list – the kind of thing a chancer could cobble together for, say, a steam-powered, light-speed hover-car. It was less a blueprint for a real product than a 'patent troll'-style legal obstacle to rivals.

After his company's early success, Henry Ford was astonished to learn of Seldon's patent and positively outraged to hear that a group of established manufacturers had used it as the basis for the formation of a trade group for automotive companies. Ford regarded the organisation as nothing less than a cartel designed to protect the cosy status quo of exclusive, expensive cars, and when taken to court over the matter in 1909 he steadfastly refused to give so much as an inch. As soon as their action began, the association of rival car firms began to place newspaper advertisements warning customers that Ford cars and parts might soon become impossible to buy and illegal to drive, and advising prospective consumers to choose one of their vehicles instead.

Over two years' effort, including an appeal, Ford won not only the case but the publicity battle while it was being fought. Later, he described it as the best advertising he'd ever had. Ford again beat them by daring to put his money behind his democratising instincts. He took out his own four-page newspaper advertisement promising any purchaser of a Ford car a bond that could be redeemed against all of Ford's assets in the event of any legal clampdown. The message was enough: according to Ford, only five customers ever took up the bond offer and, of course, the company emerged from the saga stronger than ever.

Later, Ford's rivals started trying to compete with his company's bargain price points by offering customers the opportunity to put down a deposit, commit to a long-term payment plan and drive away with a new car far fancier and more expensive than any he produced. For many years, Henry Ford, to whom debt was little short of an original sin, refused point blank to adopt such payment plans, even though his stance lost the company sales and market share.

FORD'S FAMOUS RESPONSE to the question of consumer choice – 'Any customer can have any car painted any colour that he wants so long as it's black' – perfectly encapsulated his belief that the best ideas are so democratic in conception and so efficient in delivery that the public feels obliged to vote with its wallets. By taking the cost and complexity of offering different colours out of the process of manufacturing a car, he also helped make the process of buying one feel less about choice, and more about common sense. Social equality was thereby engineered as a kind of side effect, as questions of taste and status competition were all but removed from the equation.

Ford's promise was, 'I will build a car for the great multitude.' That egalitarian vision is why he was so motivated to streamline all the complexity out of his vehicles' design, production, maintenance and repair. Only then could he hope to have access to that crucial 95 per cent – the resounding democratic majority that had the power to turn an experimental product, like his automobile, into a ubiquitous icon.

Explaining his 'magic number', Ford wrote:

> Making 'to order' instead of making in volume is, I suppose, a habit, a tradition, that has descended from the old handicraft days. Ask a hundred people how they want a particular article made. About eighty will not know; they will leave it to you. Fifteen will think that they must say something,

while five will really have preferences and reasons. The ninety-five, made up of those who do not know and admit it and the fifteen who do not know but do not admit it, constitute the real market for any product ...

The majority will consider quality and buy the biggest dollar's worth of quality. If, therefore, you discover what will give this 95 per cent of people the best all-round service and then arrange to manufacture at the very highest quality and sell at the very lowest price, you will be meeting a demand which is so large that it may be called universal.

Against today's backdrop of ever-cheaper bespoke digital production technology and affordable 3D printers, Ford's proclamations about the irrelevance of personalisation do tend to read like a rare example of him being stuck in his time. But the many lasting lessons from Ford's achievements stem from the fact that he had a dream, and was absorbed with bringing it to as many people as possible. The cars he originally made are now museum pieces, but his insights about making something of value for the masses won't rust.

Like The Beatles in their time, William Shakespeare in his, or Apple and Google today, Henry Ford knew that the greatest and most enduring kind of work a person can do is that which resonates with the most people. Rather than targeting a narrow demographic, start with the broadest possible ambition, and you stand the best chance of having the greatest cultural impact.

The Rise and Rise of
Margaret Rudkin

GOOD LEADERS ARE always smart enough to ensure they have good people around them. But – perhaps because they're so secure in their accomplishments and reputations – the very greatest leaders are often the most forthright in acknowledging how much 'their' successes have relied on other people. Not as mere enablers or assistants, implementing the vision of the 'great leader', but as irreplaceable individuals who made uniquely important contributions.

By that measure, perhaps none are greater than Margaret Rudkin, founder of Pepperidge Farm. Five years before her death, writing the story of the first quarter-century of the food brand she founded, Rudkin credited everyone but herself with its success: the husband who encouraged her to act on her daydreams; the doctors and grocers who asked her to sell them the food she fed her family; the first-ever staff member, who feared the sack after her disastrous first day yet was still at the company 25 years later, along with her entire family.

Given her proven brilliance in business, Rudkin's eagerness to acknowledge others might seem suspiciously overgenerous. She was a financial expert and a branding and a publishing pioneer. In 1960, Rudkin was described by *Who's Who* as the most important woman in US commerce. When she sold her company to the Campbell Soup Company in 1961, she continued her leadership and became the first woman to serve on the Campbell Soup Board of Directors. After her retirement she lectured at Harvard Business School. In outline, her achievements make her seem as much a master of her own fate as any legendary entrepreneur you care to think of.

But Margaret Rudkin didn't believe in the popular legend of self-made success, in the myth of the genius leader born to win. She thought that collective endeavour and serendipity were much more important than her individual destiny in the creation of a lasting business. 'I believe', she wrote, 'that success is often the result of an accidental circumstance and the opportunity to take advantage of it.' This insight probably had plenty to do with her own experience of starting a business, and with the fact that the business was food. She rose to greatness because she understood food not as a meal on a plate or a product in a package but as the material evidence of a whole web of inextricable relationships between people, places and processes.

Margaret Rudkin's professional training and life as an employee was in accountancy. Food was something she'd known the emotional importance of since childhood, but about which she lacked technical knowledge. As it became her business, she addressed this gap by talking to people

– friends, neighbours, farmers, doctors, butchers and shoppers – who had the expertise. She sought out kitchen secrets from far-flung cultures and antique cookbooks. Personal curiosity and familial necessity drove her to find out more about food, and she was ultimately able to turn the things she learned from other people into the foundations of a groundbreaking company.

By trusting in people who loved and knew about food, Rudkin gained the courage to believe in her judgement and her taste buds when she made decisions about her business, rather than allowing herself to be constrained by established food-industry conventions and assumptions. As the Pepperidge Farm's brand expanded and diversified, Rudkin's openness to other people and places remained a key factor in its success.

She had been born Margaret Fogarty in New York City in 1897 and grew up in a grand brownstone townhouse on Manhattan's Lower East Side. When Margaret was 12, her family moved to Long Island, where she flourished at both schoolwork and extra-curricular activities such as sports. On graduation she was voted class valedictorian, the student who delivers the farewell statement at the ceremony and is usually the highest ranking in their class. After graduating, she spent four years managing the accounts in a small local bank, before moving up the ladder to work on Wall Street, where she met Henry Albert Rudkin.

Margaret married Henry Rudkin in 1923, gave up her job and started a new life at home, with her increased free time allowing her to focus seriously on cookery for the first time. The 1920s were boom times for everyone on Wall Street, including Henry's brokerage firm of McClure, Jones & Co., and in 1926 the Rudkins bought 125 acres of farmland in Fairfield, Connecticut, about 50 miles northeast of Manhattan, where they built an imposing mock-Tudor manor house, complete with garages and stables to accommodate the trappings of the high-society lifestyle to which they had become accustomed. Nevertheless, they kept the homely old name 'Pepperidge Farm', which came from the local name for the sorghum trees that lined the property. Margaret later recalled that she and her family 'started our country ways like babes-in-the-wood, for neither of us knew anything about country ways.' From the moment they arrived, she made sure she addressed that by asking the people who did.

But in October 1929, everything changed. Like every other firm on Wall Street, McClure, Jones & Co. suffered a drastic change in fortune when the stock market crashed, triggering the Great Depression. Soon after, the Rudkins' personal reversal of fortune was complete when Henry, who was 12 years Margaret's senior, seriously injured himself in a polo accident that necessitated six months' convalescence. Rather than panic at this latest turn of unfortunate events, Margaret quickly rose to the challenge and quietly took control.

She immediately sold off the family's horses, and kept only one car from their fleet of automobiles. In the good times she'd spent many of her hours in the kitchen and grounds planning grand entertainments for well-heeled guests. In the bad, she reverted to her first principles to support her immediate family. The house – with its acreage, its animals and its orchards – ceased to be a stage for the Rudkins' city-slicker parties and became a vital resource. Margaret learned to make jam so that not one fruit grown on the grounds would go to waste. She talked to everyone, from the local butcher to her gardener's German wife, to learn how to cure meat and use every part of the animals she reintroduced to the farm. Eventually, thanks to her unique ingredients and booming customer-base, she even renovated and reopened the old mills on the farm that had been picturesque relics for decades before her arrival. It was the only way to get enough of the flour she needed to make her deliciously different bread.

she rose to greatness because she understood food not as a meal on a plate or a product in a package but as the material evidence of a whole web of inextricable relationships between people, places and processes.

Bread made Margaret Rudkin and her Pepperidge Farm famous, but she had to learn about baking and flour the same way she did everything else: by asking other people. And it was the needs of a person very dear to her – her son Mark – which drove her to patiently master the art of bread making, and from there found the business that is today approaching its ninth decade in operation.

The youngest of Margaret's three sons, Mark suffered badly from asthma and related allergies. In 1937, when he was eight, the Rudkins' family doctor suggested feeding him fewer pre-packaged foods and trying a diet rich in vitamin B, of which wheatgerm was one of the best-known sources. Margaret tried baking her own bread, using stoneground wholewheat flour, to see if it might better suit Mark's allergies. The initial bake though was anything but a triumph – 'My first loaf should have been sent to the Smithsonian Institution as a sample of Stone Age bread,' Rudkin later recalled, 'for it was hard as a rock and about one inch high.' But she kept working at it and her subsequent experiments and mixes of ingredients were much more successful. After much trial and error, and generous additions of honey, molasses, milk and butter, Margaret hit upon the formula for a wholewheat loaf that resulted in a delicious bread, pleasant for anyone to eat – not just because it was good for you. The bread went down well with Mark too; he seemed to digest it better than the white, sliced, store-bought variety.

From home-baker to industry leader

WHEN THE RUDKINS' family doctor saw how much progress Mark was making on his new diet, he asked about the bread. When Margaret explained her recipe, the doctor didn't believe it. It was impossible, he said, to make tasty, soft wholemeal bread without mixing in some refined white flour. So on her next visit to the doctor, she brought him some to try. Once he had, he asked Margaret to make her wholewheat bread available to his other patients too. He started prescribing it to those with similar complaints. He told fellow doctors too, and they soon sought Rudkin's bread for their own patients.

Margaret then began making trips out to bakers and markets, bringing a knife, a loaf, and a block of butter. When this anonymous 'housewife' walked into a store and asked them to stock her funny-looking brown bread it was never an easy sell. But when she cut them a slice and they tasted how good it was, the reaction was universal amazement and enthusiasm. By the time Margaret Rudkin got home from her first successful sales mission, to a grocer's in nearby Fairfield, where she had sold all of the loaves she'd brought with her, there was already a message requesting a new delivery as soon as possible.

Rudkin's new enterprise grew organically in more ways than one: moving from the kitchen to the garage, and diversifying with home-baked white bread. Because of her insistence on using unbleached flour – unknown to her suppliers – she had to reopen the old farm buildings so she could grind her own wheat on the property. Pepperidge Farm remained a local hero until a December 1939 article in *Reader's Digest* took her story nationwide. At the time, *Reader's Digest* was at the peak of its influence, with over

1.5 million US readers. Its story on Rudkin, entitled 'Bread Deluxe', championed her bread, and suggested it tapped into something much more healthy and meaningful than the bland sliced bread that had become the norm over the previous decade.

Sliced white bread had been first sold by the Chillicothe Baking Co., of Missouri. In 1928, using a machine that had been developed by inventor Otto Friedrick Rohwedder, the company marketed the new product as 'The greatest forward step in the baking industry since bread was wrapped'. That slogan was the origin of the now-familiar saying 'the best thing since sliced bread', and the ironic undercurrent it often implies. In the few short years since it first went on sale, white sliced bread had become so ubiquitous that people began to miss the old-style bread. They missed its depth of flavour, its feeling of substance and the way that – even without all the preserving agents used in the mass-produced stuff – it seemed to last longer than the new bread.

Rudkin's newfound status as a force for good in baking was both unrivalled and perfectly timed. During the US involvement in World War II, sliced bread was banned for a period on the basis that, because it required thicker plastic wrapping, it was more perishable than whole loaves and wasted precious resources. The war had helped Rudkin's cause while hampering her expansion – rationing limited supplies of many ingredients – though of course her self-sufficiency and curiosity meant she managed its privations far better than most. By late 1947, with the economy up and running again, she'd invested over $600,000 on a new factory. By moving her loyal and well-paid team of employees into the expanded premises, Rudkin's once folksy little home-baking operation had become an industrial-scale concern. From that point on, there was no looking back, as she built on her young Pepperidge Farm brand with focus and alacrity.

Sweet success

NEXT, KEEN TO diversify further, Rudkin travelled to Europe seeking inspiration. She duly returned to America as a pioneer of sweet delights, developing sophisticated continental-style biscuits and buying up a frozen pastry specialist to bring sophisticated frozen French and Danish-style treats to her compatriots' kitchens. The business got so big that Henry was now happily working full-time for his wife. While Rudkin would still insist on being the first to try every new creation, she also found time to focus on building the company's image. She extended her very personal approach to promotion by appearing in the first TV advertisements for Pepperidge Farm and enthusiastically dishing out advice on baking.

When Margaret Rudkin referred to 'marketing', she still meant what her mother had meant – going to market to buy provisions. Yet she had created the original 'anti-processed' global food brand, forging a home-grown, natural identity for her multimillion-dollar global company decades before the opening of the first Whole Foods store.

From 1956, Margaret Rudkin worked with the ad agencies of the *Mad Men* era on TV campaigns featuring Titus Moody, an appropriately crusty fictional character who travelled in a horse-drawn wagon and successfully consolidated Pepperidge Farm's rustic image.

As ever, her triumph was accompanied by unforeseen challenges; 1956 was also the year in which she underwent major surgery for breast cancer. She had no choice but to slow down – at least a little. This was no longer a little family bakery she was running. By 1960 the Pepperidge Farm workforce had numbered 1,700 and was producing 1.2 million loaves of bread per week. As such, it was a very attractive acquisition target. The Campbell Soup Company certainly thought so. In November of that year it 'bought the farm' from the Rudkins for $28 million in stock options – which was, and still is, a lot of bread.

Margaret Rudkin quickly established herself as a key director of the parent company, as well as continuing to run Pepperidge Farm, until two years later when another of her sons, William, took over the role.

In the years that she was boss, Margaret Rudkin's Pepperidge Farm enjoyed an average annual growth of 53 per cent a year. Asked for an account for her astonishing track record, Rudkin said: 'My explanation for our extraordinary growth is that Pepperidge Farm products are the best of their kind in the world.'

Between her last years in the food industry and her death in 1967, Rudkin pulled off yet another breakthrough success. In 1963, she published *The Pepperidge Farm Cookbook*, a handsomely illustrated, beautifully bound book of recipes that were so well explained and elegantly introduced that it became an instant culinary classic and the first-ever cookbook to top the *New York Times* bestseller list. The book's uncompromising production values and intricate illustrations were inspired by an antique fifteenth-century cookbook that Rudkin's staff had clubbed together to buy her as a gift after her illness. As ever, she was the first to give the credit for their contribution to her unique achievement.

Dietrich Mateschitz:

Frequent Flyer

WHEN IT IS told at all, the Red Bull story is typically told in terms of branding. It's the tale of how a premium non-alcoholic beverage – and, with it, an entire product category: the energy drink – was invented, packaged and distributed so brilliantly that Red Bull ended up all but owning the idea of adrenaline itself.

The brand has grown to embody an ethos that millions of people around the world have eagerly embraced. Its authoritative association with Formula One racing, top-flight football, record-breaking BASE jumper Felix Baumgartner and every other variety of extreme sports and endeavours constitutes an unrivalled pinnacle in modern branding. It's a definitive accomplishment, but it's not the key to the whole story. Red Bull's incredible success story actually began with a simple moment of human connection.

Until 1984, Red Bull's Austrian founder Dietrich Mateschitz was a just another high-flying marketer with a classic consumer-goods background at Unilever and Procter & Gamble.

His entrepreneurial eureka moment was a singularly democratic one. A moment in which he tried something he'd never had before and decided it was too good not to share. Others had assumed the drink he'd enjoyed wouldn't appeal to European tastes, but his own experience gave him the confidence to gamble that the proof would be in the profits.

A shot of inspiration

THE YEAR WAS 1982, and Mateschitz, then 38, had already been a branding professional for a decade, travelling far and wide to promote new pharmaceutical products from the industry's global leaders. On one such business trip to Bangkok, Mateschitz was suffering his customary acute jetlag and someone in the bar of the Mandarin Oriental Hotel recommended he try a local 'tonic drink' called Krating Daeng.

Although Krating Daeng was unknown in the West, long-distance truckers in Thailand swore by it because it helped them stay awake on the country's treacherous highways. With a degree of trepidation, Mateschitz tried a can of the stuff and soon found himself feeling alert and energised. (A sensation that, given his organisation's achievements, you suspect never left him since.)

Somebody had taken a chance that the foreign visitor might benefit from a local remedy, and it wouldn't be long before that visitor would pay the gesture forward again, on an altogether grander scale.

A few months later, this time in the Hong Kong Mandarin Oriental, Mateschitz chanced to read a newspaper article about Japan's top corporate earners. Leading the list was a company called Taisho Pharmaceutical, which manufactured over-the-counter medicines and the anti-fatigue tonic Lipovitan. The drink had been a roaring success since its launch in 1962 and had been licensed to a Thai manufacturer a few years later. Its active ingredients of caffeine, taurine and B vitamins were similar to those that made Krating Daeng so effective.

Krating Daeng itself was first introduced in 1976, by a Thai company, TC Pharmaceutical. Its founder, Chaleo Yoovidhya, had been born into a struggling family of Chinese immigrants. From an early age, in order to survive, Chaleo and his siblings had been obliged to be enterprising and entrepreneurial. It paid off, and at age 30 Yoovidhya founded TC Pharmaceutical and steadily built up a solid business distributing over-the-counter medicines. But it was his energy drink that proved to be the real driver of growth at TC Pharmaceutical. Although many other energy tonics had been released in the decade since Lipovitan was licensed to Thailand, within a year of its launch, Krating Daeng became the next most popular brand.

the way Red Bull looks at it, the company is all about networks, about the limitless potential of relationships built on shared passions.

In addition to getting the formula and flavour right, Yoovidhya had hit the mark with his unlikely-sounding choice of brand name. '*Krating daeng*' literally means 'Red gaur' – gaurs being a legendarily tough breed of bison farmed for many generations on the Thailand–Cambodia border. The thrusting bull image Yoovidhya created was a far cry from the quieter, Zen-like branding of Lipovitan and a perfect fit for the macho 'keep-on-trucking' self-image of Thai overnight drivers and shift workers. The name also nodded to the ancient origins of the drink's most magic ingredient, taurine – as it was traditionally extracted from the bile of cattle, although it has been created synthetically since the early twentieth century and is also found in eggs, meat and breast milk.

It was reading that newspaper article about the scale of Lipovitan's income that inspired Dietrich Mateschitz to transform his personal reaction of 'Why didn't someone tell me about this stuff 100 long-haul flights ago?' into a business ambition: 'If I loved it that much, why wouldn't others, everywhere?'

The Austrian-born US citizen Arnold Schwarzenegger put his finger on what was so distinctive about his country-man's (and perhaps his own) democratic instinct: 'He's a daring businessman, but for an Austrian he's also quite a visionary because he thinks in terms of the whole world.'

Mateschitz liked the Thai tonic, and he saw how others who had taken a chance on it had profited, so he decided to take it to the rest of the world. But it was important to him that he didn't simply come to that foreign land, take its best ideas, and pass them off as his own; he approached Krating Daeng's creator, Yoovidhya, directly and explained that he wanted to bring his drink to a global audience. In 1984, they entered into an equal 49 per cent partnership (the other 2 per cent went to Yoovidhya's son). Each put half a million dollars into the new Red Bull venture, and it was largely due to that deal that, when he died in March 2012, Chaleo Yoovidhya was the third richest person in Thailand.

Recipe for success

THE DEAL PLAYED to the two founders' respective strengths: Yoovidhya was responsible for formulating and manufacturing the new drink and Mateschitz was in charge of developing and distributing the brand worldwide.

The process began with a tweak to the drink's flavour, aimed at making it less alien to a European palate. Mateschitz also asked Yoovidhya to add bubbles, as in the 1980s, with the possible exception of tomato juice, tin cans meant 'fizzy drink' to European consumers, whereas Asian firms had long offered numerous still soft drinks that way.

Early taste tests on the new formula suggested that those tweaks hadn't helped much. Flavour consultants predicted a flop. Undaunted, Mateschitz knew that, unlike other soft drinks, Red Bull wasn't just about taste; it was an altogether new category of drink – one that promised improved physical and mental performance. This was the height of the era of 'taste tests', with rival colas publicly battling it out on the purely subjective question of flavour. Mateschitz ignored the crowd and calmly set about redefining what the limits of a soft drink could be and how it could be sold.

Mateschitz's egalitarian, open approach to individuals and experience helped fast-track his company to the status of global giant.

He spent two more years painstakingly refining the marketing master plan that would communicate this message, before finally launching Red Bull in Austria on 1 April 1987. He first cultivated an air of maverick excitement and edginess around the product, then steered the maturation of the brand's image as it became established in chiller cabinets everywhere. The open-endedness of the drink's simple slogan – 'Gives you wings' – enabled Mateschitz to move far beyond rave culture and extreme stunts and into elite sports, music and communications media.

Long before other brands understood how important owning media channels would soon become, Mateschitz also established Red Bull's many communications vehicles. Red Bull recognised how new online technologies were democratising publishing and foresaw that many existing forms of media would become fragmented, taking audience, power and influence away from old gatekeepers. The best new brands like Red Bull would have to maintain their profile and connection with people by being their own publishers, content creators and editors – by establishing their own new networks of mutual interest. Ingeniously, Red Bull magazines, TV stations, shows and digital channels were never about hard-selling the product. They started out as they remain: covering stories and sporting events for people who crave extreme excitement and fast-lane living.

Mateschitz – an adrenaline junkie who had supported himself through his business studies by working as a ski instructor – largely bypassed conventional advertising. Instead, he set about building global links to those dedicated to the thrill of extreme human endeavour and performance. Today, the brand invests in football teams on three continents. It owns a fleet of vintage air-display planes and sponsors countless extreme sports events, concerts and competitions. The Formula One team Mateschitz bought in 2006 when it was a lowly also-ran went on to produce the youngest F1 champion driver in the competition's history.

It's an achievement, built on a far-sighted understanding of how to connect and communicate the brand equity of an energy drink with thrill seekers all around the world. Yet from Mateschitz's perspective on his global marketplace, it was no more than a logical step in keeping with the DNA of his brand.

In other words, when you know why you're doing what you're doing, and when you have faith that others will feel the same way, there's no need to overcomplicate your message. Reach out and clearly communicate the things that move you, and give like-minded people every incentive to respond faster and more strongly to become advocates and allies of your brand and its message.

The network ethic

IN AN IMPRESSIVELY far-sighted paper written in 1997, for a title called *The Technology Management Handbook*, two Stanford professors and another from Berkeley Haas School of Business wrote that entrepreneurs are 'social creatures, not solo heroes'. Tom Byers, Heleen Kist and Robert Sutton contended that the conventional picture of great entrepreneurs as 'one-person-wonders', as favoured in business books since the 1950s, was a romantic one. They suggested that this was based on the human need to pick out a causal agent as the hero behind the events we witness to make sense of them, when the reality is much more complicated.

If you stop looking at business from the single perspective of brilliant individuals, the academics argued, a different picture emerges. Successful leaders were often so because they were highly empathetic; social networks have always been essential to business. They wrote:

> Building a company entails hiring, organizing, and inspiring a collection of people who typically need to get start-up

funds from others, to buy things from other people, and ultimately, flourish or fail together as a result of the ability to sell things to yet another group of people. The emphasis on rugged individualism is so prevalent in western culture that many of the lists of 'characteristics of successful entrepreneurs' barely reflect that launching a start-up entails constant interaction with others.

Before online social networks, before networking meant swapping business cards or adding a colleague on LinkedIn, these leaders connected with people, and each connection they made led to a whole set of opportunities and encounters.

The way Red Bull looks at it, the company is all about networks, about the limitless potential of relationships built on shared passions. It's an orchestra creating a networked, independent harmony – not a single salesman banging the same drum over and over again. It's markedly different from the traditional way packaged goods companies have gone about things – where the model is becoming unwieldy, more expensive, fragmented and less effective.

Mateschitz's egalitarian, open approach to individuals and experience helped fast-track his company to the status of global giant.

Since the company was founded, over 40 billion cans of Red Bull have been consumed. That number equates to almost six cans for every person on the planet. An astonishing number – though perhaps not to Dietrich Mateschitz.

Today, admiring entrepreneurs the world over can only look on in wonder at the Red Bull story, and repeat what Mateschitz said back in the beginning: 'I'll have whatever he's drinking.'

Bill Gates:

The Numbers Man

SOME 40 YEARS after Microsoft's foundation, it's too easy to forget the connection between the philosophies of Bill Gates the software mogul and Bill Gates the philanthropist. Historians of the digital revolution often neglect to credit the fact that some of Microsoft's greatest moves under Gates were about reaching out to the masses.

In a latter-day version of Herbert Hoover's election promise of, 'a chicken in every pot and a car in every garage', Bill Gates had a clear vision of his own. He wanted to see 'a computer on every desk and in every home', and he pursued that aim with characteristic discipline and focus. As a computer software mogul he was able to change and influence the lives of so many people because he set more store in the numbers than in his own myth or ego. As a philanthropist and fund-raiser, he's applied the same logic to change the lives of many millions more.

IT WAS STEVE Jobs who, in 2007, conceded that Bill 'built the first software company before anybody really in our industry knew what a software company was'. Part of the reason Gates could see into our future was his prodigious talent for mathematics and a relentless thirst for know-ledge. His numbers were astonishing as soon as anybody started measuring them – he graduated from school with a points score of 1,590 out of 1,600 (99.4 per cent). Before he dropped out of Harvard, Gates wrote a pancake-sort-ing algorithm in record time in a timed trial in his combinatorics class. For 30 years after he left, it remained the fastest ever student solution to the problem.

Being obsessed with 'winning business' isn't the same as being obsessed with money. Indeed, Gates's obsession with number-crunching problems out of existence prob-ably owed as much to his prodigious natural affinity for the problem-solving processes of writing and correcting computer code as to any more material concerns. A natural -born problem-solver, Gates prefers to make the kind of difference he can see clearly in the data to the kind of ques-tions that get in the way of getting on with things.

During the first five years of Microsoft's existence, Gates is said to have checked every single line of code written at the company. It's hard to exaggerate how much his scrutiny of causes and effects – his unsparing eye for quality control, efficiency and effectiveness, for proven and measurable results over self-regarding assumptions – inspired colleagues and rivals alike. When the numbers are your only objective and you pursue them absolutely and without distraction, you leave performance norms in the dust.

Big bets

MICROSOFT'S SOFTWARE JUGGERNAUTS provided new ways of communicating and new standards for transferring information. Even the names Gates gave his software smash hits were unambiguous, accessible and memorable: Windows; Word; Excel; Access; Office. PowerPoint introduced a universal presentation system that, regardless of whether you loved it or loathed it, advocated new standards of brevity and clarity that crept into every kind of company and institution and shaped the way we communicated digitally in the 1990s as much as Twitter does today.

Microsoft's CD-ROM-based digital encyclopaedia project, Encarta, was never so widely used by so many. It was a bold and optimistic endeavour in its day – a statement of dedication to extending knowledge. Had it arrived in the online era, rather than the inaccessible, cumbersome disc-based digital world that preceded it, Encarta might have had a chance of becoming something as widely available as Wikipedia – which truly democratised the potential of the public to contribute to the cultural record – rather than merely inspiring it. Given its uncomplicated software code base, Wikipedia proved that digital democracy is more a social revolution than a technological one.

In 1997, when Microsoft bought a webmail start-up called Hotmail, Gates's company not only brought free email to the masses, but also invented the idea of viral marketing by tagging a signature welcoming new applicants to Hotmail with every message. Every recipient of a note through the service became a potential route to it.

Four years after the acquisition of Hotmail, in the last grand project green-lit by Gates, Microsoft launched its first videogame console, and the Xbox became a success in the US and Europe, disrupting the videogame industry's established players and setting new standards for online gameplay and networked services in the process.

The Gates to Google

IN JANUARY 1996, California's Stanford University opened a pristine new state-of-the-art building for its computing faculty. The existence of the new facility was thanks in part to a $6-million donation from the technology entrepreneur whose name was carved in stone above its entrance. A group of Stanford PhD students were the first to get to use the well-appointed computer lab in the William Gates Computer Science Building, and James Gibbons, dean of the engineering school, boldly predicted:

Within the next 18 months something will happen here, and there will be some place, some office, some corner, where people will point and say, 'Yeah, that's where they worked on the fill-in-the-blank in 1996 and 1997'.

But just how significant that 'something' would be is almost beyond imagination.

Two of those PhD students started work right away to build a better search engine. The pair loved and were keen to continue their studies, but were obsessed with making online searches smarter, so, although the project wasn't driven by the urge to start a business, as their work developed they found themselves at the head of one. The domain name of that business, Google.com, was registered in September 1997.

Larry Page and Sergey Brin's search engine was a revelation – first in the way it looked and then in the way it worked. Its democratic devotion to making things faster and more readily accessible was self-evident. Google's subsequent efforts to make all the knowledge in the world immediately available to all stemmed from that original quest to provide better access to information. There was one Internet before you first googled, and another one after it.

While Page and Brin rightfully get the credit for opening up the Internet's frontiers to us all, Bill Gates's part in their technologically enabled democratisation of information isn't always acknowledged. Larry and Sergey's search engine project started in the very space he had designed to foster such experiments.

A global legacy

IN JANUARY OF 2000, five years after making the donation that helped build the place where Google was born, Bill Gates stepped back from the day-to-day running of Microsoft. Gates remained chairman and assumed the newly created position of chief software architect. In 2006, Gates announced that he would switch to working part-time for Microsoft and full-time for the Bill & Melinda Gates Foundation, the fund for healthcare and education work that he founded with his wife. And Bill Gates, the twentieth-century captain of industry and now the twenty-first-century philanthropist, is still most at home in the realm of numbers. Statistics might not *always* be the best way of gauging the value of your effect on people's lives, but they are a pretty solid, and relatively objective, start.

In financial negotiations over the supply of medicines, pharmaceutical companies are usually seen as the power players in the US, because there's no regulation of their price points, meaning the most sought-after treatments can command astronomical prices. But Gates, with that ever-attentive eye on the effectiveness of his output and the efficiency of his spending, has driven audacious deals to secure top-quality vaccines at bargain-basement rates.

Every inoculation counts, especially since the Bill & Melinda Gates Foundation's vaccination programmes against diseases such as malaria aim to ultimately eradicate them forever. Working with the World Health Assembly's Global Polio Eradication Initiative, the Foundation has already been a key part of the vaccination push that has seen cases of the disease decrease by 99 per cent world-wide. In most of the handful of countries where there are still cases of polio, the annual numbers of cases are already down to double figures, and shrinking by half with each passing year. Those countries, which include Nigeria and Afghanistan, are now being helped by the Foundation to learn from the experience of officials in India, where the disease has finally been eliminated.

In their annual letter to supporters for 2014, Bill and Melinda pointed out that although the preponderance of news reporting tends to gives the impression that the world is getting worse, the numbers prove that people are actually living longer and healthier lives today than at any other time in history. Over $30 billion has gone directly to charitable causes because of the Bill & Melinda Gates Foundation, and the couple's pride in its effectiveness and future legacy is self-evident from the fact that it bears their names.

But just as it's difficult to overestimate the scale of this outreach, it's also hard to exaggerate quite how inspira-tionally unaffected Gates is about his own ego and image as a great entrepreneur or historical figure. In 1994, he paid $30.8 million at auction for a notebook of original manuscripts and drawings by Leonardo da Vinci – making it the most expensive manuscript in the world. When asked which he'd preserve in a fire, his business legacy or the da Vinci documents, he didn't hesitate to say he'd make sure Leonardo survived.

The Tomorrow People

LIMITLESS IDEAS EMPOWER limitless numbers of people. In the contemporary global marketplace, it goes without saying that this is good for business. But, done in good faith, it's also good for the people – especially now. The old model of representation said that democracy was something we delegated to professionals in cloistered chambers in faraway cities. Nowadays, digital networks allow us, all of us, to speak to each other remotely and to those in power as we represent ourselves by ourselves. In every facet of business, politics and social life, we can see the changes this shift has wrought to the way each of us sees and lives in the world.

Because ours is a time when we are alternately battered and anaesthetised by ubiquitous messages, we all crave 'authenticity' and seek more meaningful connections. We are more primed than ever to appreciate and advocate for businesses that are willing to make an all-out commitment to something. We want them to share the things they love, and to tell us from the heart about why they matter too.

If a leader is sincerely driven by the urge to share something, by the idea that a product deserves a much wider audience, then it's not only the culture around them that they will change. When they can successfully communicate and share their sense of mission with their staff as well as their public, such leaders tend naturally to cultivate more egalitarian, mutually respectful corporate cultures too.

if you really believe in something, you've never had more reason to try to find out if others do too.

Warm, fluffy feelings aside, there's a second, purely structural reason why committed democratisers have even more to gain in business in the age of digital. As the stories of Margaret Rudkin and Dietrich Mateschitz remind us – and as the before-and-after numbers for Bill Gates's outreach projects, from university bequests to vaccination programmes, prove – human networks have always been at the core of democratic entrepreneurialism. The stronger and broader the human networks with which you connect, the more confidently you can launch a product that nobody has focused-grouped, road-tested or imagined before. When there's no formal precedent for your plan, you can either retreat in fear, or see what ordinary people make of what you offer them.

Networks have always been the key to doing democratising business, but before digital they were slow-burning things that grew at the speed of word-of-mouth. Advantages were slowly conveyed from neighbour to neighbour, village to town, region to nation. What many of the most striking business models of our time have done is use technology to convert these latent networks into instant, interconnected and worldwide forces.

Whether offering cab services, accommodation, or just new ways to socialise with people, these digital-era democratising propositions do not need to do the infra-structural groundwork and bricks-and-mortar investment that equivalent analogue-era businesses did. Digital companies don't even need to excel at building new tech-nologies. Their appeal and rocketing market valuations happened because they are so good at combining existing technologies and networks, not because they invent their own. Their ingenuity comes in the way they interconnect and aggregate those digital networks that are already out there.

Then and now, from the Model T to the app-enabled cab, successful democratic offerings stand for one and the same truth, one we should all be mindful of: that making something you believe in as widely accessible as possible makes the world look better for everybody, not just your accounts department.

Today, we can all access the kinds of digital tools on which those latest network-savvy companies were founded. We can take a chance on reaching out, and do it with less outlay of time, money and resources than ever. Digital gives you innumerable opportunities to take a chance that people might want to try what you like. You can get an idea to your public, and let them vote with their wallets to Kickstart it into reality. If the right social-media giant or technology titan likes what you offer, your idea can go from an unknown quantity to a mass-media phenomenon in hours. If you really believe in something, you've never had more reason to try to find out if others do too. Targeting preordained demographics might make you money, at least for a time, but democratising will make you something much more meaningful than that.

the stronger and broader the human networks with which you connect, the more confidently you can launch a product that nobody has focused-grouped, road-tested or imagined before. When there's no formal precedent for your plan, you can either retreat in fear, or see what ordinary people make of what you offer them.

Revolutionise

How impossible dreams

power practical success.

'Revolutionary'

THE WAY WE regard that word at any given time tells us a lot about the status quo of the day. If you were a believer in the old establishments in the early twentieth century, a 'revolutionary' was a dangerous person hell-bent on ruining society. If you were a dutiful citizen in the Soviet Union after 1917, 'revolutionary' was a word applied to everything as a drab seal of state endorsement – to the extent that if it was not 'revolutionary' it was probably banned.

But in the West today, with memories of the bloody revolts of the twentieth century becoming evermore distant, 'revolutionary' usually indicates something new and exciting. This change in our perception of the word 'revolution' shows how receptive about and eager for new ideas people are right now.

The revolutionaries whose stories are told in this chapter have all been indispensable examples to me because they all found ways to get beyond the all-consuming cultural conventions of their times. They discovered new ways of thinking about business and breaking through the boundaries of what their peers considered possible.

they achieve their impossible dreams by being
uncommonly aware of and alert to the people and
society around them. It's their humanity, humility
and receptiveness, their willingness to change their
tactical approaches, that allows them to achieve their
strategic goals.

That's what makes revolutionaries: a stubborn belief that the world, or some corner of it, doesn't *have* to be the way it is and enough raw conviction to dedicate their lives to proving it.

This is also a key characteristic of the entrepreneurial mindset. After all, disruption can only happen if you're willing to question convention and consensus in the first place.

Legendary founders who have established Limitless businesses first discovered success by thinking beyond accepted norms. Then, their companies stayed on top by continuing to swim upstream – forever questioning industry-standard assumptions about growth, distribution and customer expectations.

It takes a rebel to lead a revolution. But a rebel isn't just someone who resists control or convention. Rebels think differently; they look at things differently and then act in correspondence with this change of thought. They aim to influence the future against conformist authority and revolt in the face of narrow-minded rigidity. As the stories in this chapter demonstrate, rebels are visionaries who open doors to new perception.

Business leaders need the ability to see what should change and have the compulsion to realise it. But the greatest business revolutionaries aren't usually megalomaniacs set on making the world work the way it should in their heads. On the contrary, they achieve their impossible dreams by being uncommonly aware of and alert to the people and society around them. It's their humanity, humility and receptiveness, their willingness to change their tactical approaches, that allows them to achieve their strategic goals.

Humility isn't a quality you normally associate with revolutionaries, but it's what allowed Akio Morita to found Sony from the ashes of Japan's wartime defeat. Humility is perhaps one of the reasons that, on his return to Apple, Steve Jobs went from being a brilliant inventor to a revolutionary leader. The challenge Jobs faced with his second start-up, NeXT, and the Pixar transformation he

when you have an outsider's perspective and are forced to learn the workings of an alien society in order to get by, your lack of learned assumptions about 'the rules' can be turned to your business advantage.

led equipped him with a much-enhanced ability to adapt, rethink and listen – in addition to providing the foundations of Apple's now ubiquitous ecosystem.

Steve Jobs was raised by adoptive parents. Akio Morita came of age in an old country newly occupied and controlled by a foreign army. It's perhaps no accident that, in one way or another, an outsized proportion of entrepreneurs have 'outsider' backgrounds. We know the children of immigrants frequently do disproportionately well as entrepreneurs, as do many people with 'disabilities' such as dyslexia or Asperger's syndrome. When you have an outsider's perspective and are forced to learn the workings of an alien society in order to get by, your lack of learned assumptions about 'the rules' can be turned to your business advantage. You respond to what you see, not what you're told. And if you have the advantage of growing up with two cultures and two (or more) languages from the start, you learn early in life how distinctly different societies serve to define our single world. You see intuitively how many of our limitations are superimposed on the world by people, rather than being eternally true; you know, long before you first hear the phrase, that, 'the map is not the territory'.

The first engineers built the first bridges. In tribal societies, an analytical problem-solver who questioned collective beliefs would be an outlier in the tribe. When they came to a river that their peers regarded as the impassable edge of their known universe, these engineering-minded outliers didn't see it as a barrier, but as an opportunity. Through diligent work and trial and error, they built crossings that changed the perceptions of their fellow villagers, expanding the conceptual threshold of their world by physically extending it. These engineers were assets to their tribes despite their abnormal preoccupations, because those odd obsessions eventually brought benefits for all.

by getting beyond the particulars of their own specific cultures and times, these leaders were not only better equipped to create revolutionary change but were also better positioned to adapt when it was thrust upon them.

In many respects, human culture has changed more quickly in the last few hundred years than it did over the many millennia before. But that principle – of the revolutionary who sees a new horizon before anybody else, and then works to share that vision with the rest of society – still applies.

There are more revolutionary entrepreneurs than there are Limitless businesses. That's because the human understanding needed to introduce and iterate great products or services is just as rare a quality as great engineering aptitude. If both attributes are abundant in a single individual or institution, they provide once-in-a-generation potential for sustained accomplishment.

The more I've dug into the stories behind the diverse lives of the leaders I admire the most, the more I believe that, for all their differing experiences and achievements, there are many recurring themes to their stories.

Of these themes, the most striking to me is how, whether by choice or experience, revolutionary leaders often seem to have had some kind of epiphany or insight early on – a moment of revelation that gave them a glimpse of a world far different to that which life seemed to have been preparing for them. This other world they'd glimpsed was somehow bigger, broader and more pregnant with possibility than the one that most people are resigned to accept.

this chapter's heroes, never happy in their comfort zones, all found their own ways to channel the ebb and flow of events, instead of being restrained by rigid oppositions and abstract ideals.

It seemed to me that this sense enabled these leaders to look beyond the limited destinies that societal norms may have had in mind for them, and to put their faith in technologies for which others believed the world had no use. By getting beyond the particulars of their own specific cultures and times, these leaders were not only better equipped to create revolutionary change but were also better positioned to adapt when it was thrust upon them.

Friedrich Nietzsche once wrote about the possibility of 'higher-level thinking'. Nietzsche argued that most people cannot attain higher-level thinking because they're held back by the basic conceptual limits that were once vital to human survival. In our earliest tribal societies, he argued, the conceptual and linguistic habit of dividing the world into opposites – light and dark, good and bad, master and servant – allowed communities to survive and ward off danger by simplifying their experience into the purely positive and the purely negative. Once you'd survived an encounter with one hungry tiger or one angry non-native tribesman, you made sure you didn't give any of them the benefit of the doubt again. From that day forth, to ensure the survival of your own group, you automatically assumed all unfamiliar tribes to be enemies.

For Nietzsche, that ancient survival strategy had become a cultural handicap. Though science had shown that the world was in a process of constant change, our old fixed ideas about rigid opposites, a relic 'of the most rudimentary human psychology', still dominated our thinking. As far as he was concerned, humans still have 'a habit of seeing opposites ... where there are not opposites, but only differences of degree'. He said:

> An unspeakable amount of painfulness, arrogance, harshness, estrangement and frigidity has entered into human affairs because we think we see opposites instead of transitions.

Nietzsche said that the standard, unexamined conceptual oppositions, 'the basic presuppositions of the metaphysics of reason', still operated on the same principle as ancient tribal cults: as a bit of would-be magic, invoked as a source of comfort, and an illusory indicator of human power in the face of the might of nature.

This chapter's heroes, never happy in their comfort zones, all found their own ways to channel the ebb and flow of events, instead of being restrained by rigid oppositions and abstract ideals. When they succeeded, they not only saw beyond the inherited ideas of their worlds but they also worked out brilliant, adaptive ways to share their far-sighted visions with their customers and their colleagues.

Thomas Edison:
Ingenious Invention

OUR FIRST TWO stories tell the parallel lives of two arch-tinkerers, born 7,000 miles and over half a century apart. From an early age both were quite extraordinary electronic engineers, and neither was willing to compromise his vision to succeed in the world of commerce.

One of these revolutionary thinkers, Thomas Edison, laid the foundations for much of our modern world with an astonishing sequence of inventions and experiments. The other, Akio Morita, broke with family and national tradition by subsuming his name and identity to that of the new kind of business he wanted to set up. Over his subsequent 48 years in charge, he built one of most trusted and powerful brands in the world.

The lone ranger

THOMAS EDISON WAS a tireless experimenter. With the incandescent light bulb, he outpaced and improved on the thoughts of all the inventors before him and revolutionised a 50-year-old idea to produce a reliable, long-lasting, safe, practical, economical and scalable source of light. As Paul

Israel wrote in his definitive biography *Edison: A Life of Invention*:

> But the electric light was not a single invention emanating from an inspired genius. Instead it was a complex network of inventions produced by one of the first institutions of organised corporate research. As he invented a system of electric lighting, Edison was simultaneously reinventing the system of invention ... While Edison the individual is celebrated as the inventor of the electric light, it was the less visible corporate organisation of laboratory and business enterprise that enabled him to succeed.

Thomas Edison's Menlo Park complex, a 34-acre site, which he called 'The Invention Factory', was among the first and most recognised institutions of organised research and development. In this site Edison revolutionised R&D and proved to be an effective manager of innovation and innovators by empowering his teams to deliver a continuous stream of ideas and improvements.

Over 400 patents were applied for at Menlo Park, including one for the phonograph, the first machines for playing back recorded sound. Relentless in his pursuits, Edison also described an idea for a device that would: 'do for the eye what the phonograph does for the ear' in another filing with the patent office. This invention, known as the 'Kinetoscope', would become standard for cinematic projection before the advent of video.

Thomas Edison also masterminded the distinctive application of celebrity to business by becoming the world's most famous inventor. A six-part film documentary, known as *A day with Thomas Edison*, recorded in New Jersey in 1922 witnesses the 74-year-old Edison's leadership, collaborations and conversations, noting:

> his experiments and inventions, the results of which have been so far-reaching and beneficial to mankind, now give employment to more than a million people.

With his astonishing foresight in a fast-changing era, Edison won the Grand Prize at the Universal Exposition in Paris, where he was described as 'Inventor of the age'. Today Edison is also known as 'the most influential figure of our millennium'.

Fascinating and inspirational, Edison was also intriguing and complex. His revolutionary spirit (demonstrated by his 1,093 patents) wasn't matched by an enthusiasm for dealing with more mature phases of the industry that he had helped to create. At one stage or another, whether with light, sound, moving image or electricity, Edison was in the driver's seat to dominate every one of these emerging fields that today sustain and stimulate our existence. Yet, one by one, especially when it challenged the dominance of the technology he invented, he missed opportunities to capitalise on his inventions and take an enduring lead in the new markets he'd created.

In the beginning, Edison, who in 1847 was born in the small town of Milan, Ohio, was certainly one bright spark. The last of seven children born to his mother, Nancy, his story bears the hallmarks of classic entrepreneurial origins. Thomas's parents were recent immigrants from Canada and had the kind of zeal for self-improvement that saw his mother read literary classics to him at bedtime and bring him his first science book when he was just nine years old.

The young Thomas was an archetypal outsider in other ways too. In his entire childhood, he managed only three months of organised schooling, every day of which he hated. Despite later bringing music to the masses, he was partially deaf, having started to lose his hearing in his teens – one of those supposed 'disabilities' that, according to Edison, were anything but a limitation. On the contrary, he maintained it enabled him to shut out 'all the foolish conversation and meaningless sound that normal people hear' and to focus on his higher aims.

Those aims included undertaking experiments and trying to make money. At 11, by which time the Edison family had moved to Michigan in search of better fortunes, Thomas had begun growing and selling fruit and vegetables. He soon realised however that he could buy in produce from outside the town and sell them on at a greater profit. The fruit stall he set up enabled him to give his mother the grand sum of a dollar a day.

Perhaps that early success helped Thomas win her over the following year, when she agreed to bring an end to his home schooling so that he could take a job selling newspapers to passengers on the train to Detroit.

While this incident may have endangered lives, it was the saving of one that led to Edison's next adventure.

Newsworthy beginnings

EDISON'S FIRST REVOLUTIONARY business innovation came in April 1862 while he was still in his newspaper-selling job. The American Civil War was at its height, and Thomas was in his sixteenth year. One morning, before setting off for the train to sell newspapers, Thomas made a detour to the offices of the *Detroit Free Press*, where he talked his way into the plant and checked the lead stories for the latest editions. He then wired the attention-grabbing headlines ahead, to each of the train stations on his route. The Battle of Shiloh, one of the pivotal events of the Civil War, was being waged, and Edison knew people were hungry for updates by the fastest available method: the newspaper. By the time Edison arrived on the train himself, hot-off-the-press copies of the day's paper in hand, he had a ready-made queue of eager customers awaiting the full story.

The Shiloh wire-wheeze was a one-off that made the most of extraordinary circumstances. Rather than attempt to repeat the trick for diminishing returns, Edison used the extra money it had generated to buy a basic letterpress and 300 pounds of newsprint paper.

He quickly taught himself to set moving type, with which newspaper pages were laid out, assiduously gathering all the gossip he could from his gregarious days on the train and in the town. He then promptly started up his own weekly newspaper, stocked full of information local to his route, complete with reckless libels and abundant spelling mistakes but full of things you would never see in the newspapers from Detroit, or for that matter anywhere else.

The change from selling somebody else's daily newspaper to selling his own weekly left Edison with more time to himself on the train. With his letterpress rig on board, he could quickly print extra copies on demand when stocks ran low.

Having secured this revolutionary piece of moving real estate for his printing operation, Edison next proposed to the train's guard that he be allowed to push the favour even further and establish a mobile laboratory in the last carriage. This would mean that, rather than wasting valuable time idling as the train ran back and forth between Detroit and Port Huron, he could instead do scientific experiments.

Working with phosphorus one day, Edison accidentally set the lab-carriage on fire. Fearful for his own job, the guard he'd brokered the arrangement with unceremoniously ejected Edison, his printing press and what remained of his laboratory and paper supply from the train.

While this incident may have endangered lives, it was the prevention of another incident with a train that led to Edison's next adventure. He had been sitting close to the telegraph instruments in railroad offices to learn Morse code, and he noticed that the station agent James MacKenzie's young son was playing on the tracks, unaware that a freight car was rolling towards him. Edison rescued the whippersnapper, simply declaring: 'I luckily came out just in time'. Grateful for his heroism, MacKenzie taught Edison Morse code with such intensity that he was able to become a professional telegraph operator. It wasn't long before he went from operator to inventor.

The record breaker

TELEGRAPHY WAS EDISON'S core expertise and that day's pre-eminent high-tech field. Alexander Graham Bell invented the first practical telephone, being awarded the US patent in 1876. Edison – who was the same age as Bell – set about improving upon Bell's exciting new concept, and revolutionised it with a series of indispensible improvements. These included a new kind of receiver and the carbon transmitter that captured sound better than the previous magnetic design. While tinkering with the telephone, Edison was able to invent the phonograph in 1877 – the first device to reproduce recorded sound.

On the day that the 15-year-old Edison wired the news headlines to commuters waiting down the line, he had pretty much invented what today is known as a 'Rich Site Summary' (RSS) feed – only he did it 140 years earlier in the age of steam. And 19 years later, in 1888, having pioneered so much in recorded sound, Edison built on the ground-breaking sequential photographic studies of Eadweard Muybridge to create a similar record-and-playback system for images. Throughout his life Edison enjoyed telling stories and collecting jokes. Perhaps that's why the very first films the US public ever paid to see were his employees' stutter-ing, 20-second loops of amusing or exciting happenings.

Those first Edison Manufacturing Company films were made by a Scotsman, William Dickson. An avid photog-rapher, Dickson had also greatly helped Edison in the development of the first 'Kinetoscope' film camera and the invention of celluloid film.

At the urging of two boxing promoters, Dickson stum-bled on the lucrative idea of filming a six-round fight and charging the public to watch each 60-second reel. This effec-tively gave birth to the first cinematic cliffhanger, the episodic drama and the concept of pay-per-view all in one fell swoop.

Within 15 years, as Edison's labs developed reels of film that could run for 10 minutes or more, Edwin Porter, the talented early film pioneer based in New York and a director with the Edison Manufacturing Company, laid down the grammar of Hollywood movies – only this was 1902, and Hollywood didn't yet exist.

Edison eventually turned his back on movies altogether. By that time, rebel moviemakers had fled to the West coast, and an arid area of the Californian desert they dubbed 'Hollywoodland', to avoid the punitive licensing fees from patents, in much the same way as top directorial talent had left to find partners whose moviemaking ambitions matched their own.

By 1911 Thomas Edison revealed his vision to make learning more engaging with films for schools that would teach children:

> everything, from mathematics to morality, by little dramas acted out before the camera, and reproduced in the school-room at very low cost. Sort o' swing the education in on them so attractively that they'll want to go to school.

Current affairs

THE FIRST ERA of electric cars arrived in 1890, and in 1900, 28 per cent of the cars built in the US were electric. One of the early pioneers, the Detroit Electric Car Company, manufactured around 13,000 vehicles between 1907 and 1939. Even though they advertised 80 miles between charges, an endurance run of 211 miles was reached on a single battery charge. Thomas Edison's batteries powered these automobiles. He said:

> Electricity is the thing. There is no whirring and grinding gears with the numerous levers to confuse. There is not that almost terrifying uncertain throb and whirr of the power-

ful combustion engine. There is no water circulating the system to get out of order – no dangerous and evil-smelling gasoline and no noise.

Sales of electric cars fell in the 1920s as internal-combustion-engine automobiles became less expensive, more roads got built and people travelled greater distances. But in 1914, Henry Ford gave the only interview in which he admitted in *The New York Times* that he and Thomas Edison had been working on an electric automobile 'which would be cheap and practicable'. Ford said:

> The problem so far has been to build a storage battery of light weight which would operate for long distances without recharging.

According to the terms of the deal, Ford's electric car would run exclusively with Edison's batteries and, until the plan came unstuck, Ford was due to buy 100,000 of them. Unfortunately however, Edison's nickel-iron batteries turned out to lack the capacity to reliably power a car, so, the company replaced them with more powerful – but also much heavier – lead-acid batteries. While the batteries now performed, the cars were overburdened by the extra weight, and hopelessly slow to drive. The project came to an abrupt end.

Ever devoted to the business of innovation, Edison was also fascinated by the potential of iron ore. The movie and music-making profits his companies earned in the 1880s and 1890s helped bail out the iron-ore mining operation he'd been working on since 1870. Edison finally left the iron business in 1899, but not before he'd inadvertently discovered that he could sell the waste sand from his ore milling process to cement manufacturers. This piqued his interest and he took to investigating how he might transfer his rock-crushing techniques to cement production. Over the next few years Edison came up with a number of major innovations, including a rotary kiln that he licensed to other cement manufacturers. One of Edison's lesser-known legacies was the old Yankee Stadium in New York City (demolished in 2008) that was built in 1922 with 45,000 barrels of concrete supplied by the Edison Portland Cement Company.

The application of technology to find solutions to social problems is evident through Edison's idea of affordable cement housing for low-income families. He even developed plans for a system of casting a house in half a day from iron moulds. In October 1907 he announced:

> I have not gone into this with the idea of making money from it, and will be glad to license reputable parties to make moulds and erect houses without any payments on account of patents. The only restriction is that the design of the houses be satisfactory to me, and that they should use good material.

DESPITE THE MASSIVE capitalisation of the industries that Edison helped to create, his estate was estimated to be worth only $12 million at the time of his death in 1931. However, even Edison's measure of what constituted prosperity was more revolutionary than mere monetary gain: 'Anything that won't sell, I don't want to invent. Its sale is proof of utility, and utility is success.'

Edison's appetite for his work and new possibilities was Limitless. Not one to put much emphasis on the present, his fondness was for what was next and unstated future needs. His work ethic and relentless desire to experiment was a greater motivation than fully realising his innovations' financial potential. As he said:

> One might think that the money value of an invention constitutes its reward ... I continue to find my greatest pleasure, and so my reward, in the work that precedes what the world calls success.

A true revolutionary, Edison determined that 'discontent' is 'the first necessity of progress'. His famous quote 'I've not failed. I've just found 10,000 ways that won't work' was a typically inspiring way of encouraging experimentation. The trailblazing ideas that sprung from his leadership, and his somewhat unique cognitive style of being able to make leaps between diverse fields, made a singularly influential and triumphant contribution to science.

But perhaps the story that best encapsulates the indomitable spirit of Thomas Alva Edison comes from one of the many destructive fires he suffered over the years. At around 5.30 in the evening of 10 December 1914, a massive explosion shook Edison's film plant in West Orange, New Jersey. Fuelled by the chemicals within, more than half the site was engulfed in flames in what witnesses claimed to be a matter of minutes. According to a *Reader's Digest* account of what followed, on observing the inferno, Edison called out to his 24-year-old son Charles, 'Go get your mother and all her friends. They'll never see a fire like this again.' Later that night as the fire still smouldered he told a *New York Times* reporter, 'Although I'm over 67 years old I'll start all over again tomorrow' – and he did.

Akio Morita:

Revolutionary Ronin

IT WAS THOMAS Edison who said, 'Vision without execution is hallucination.' It was Akio Morita who proved him right.

Morita was born in 1921, ten years before Edison's death. He grew up as part of a well-heeled and unusually well-travelled family in Nagoya, Japan, steeped in old learning, entrenched privilege and responsibility. If Edison's electrical entrepreneurialism began as a quest to make his name and make some money for his family, Morita's own drive was partly about escaping the legacy of his name and inherited wealth. His vision was of a new kind of company for a drastically different country and an utterly changed post-war world. His focus on execution built an organisation that, at its peak, achieved an undefeated brand loyalty and enduring presence in people's lives.

Morita saw technology not just as a power to be harnessed by great men in grand projects for the betterment of humankind but also as a domestic force for bringing pleasure and practical, everyday empowerment to individual people. He believed that technology could be usefully looked at in terms of luxury and self-expression, not just necessity and power consumption. It was a vision that his company, Sony, would go on to communicate through its products for decades.

The 1920s Japan into which Morita was born was still run along almost feudal lines, where a select few high-born samurai families were allowed to own land and run state-sanctioned businesses according to a system called *zaibatsu*. As the firstborn son, it was taken for granted that Akio would eventually take over the family business – a producer of soy sauce, miso and sake – thereby taking the Morita family *zaibatsu* (which literally translates as 'wealth clique' but means a large family-controlled business conglomerate) into its fifteenth successive generation. But young Akio, who from his earliest days, like many other Limitless leaders, was an expert electronic experimenter, had other ideas.

Although his vision of the future was dramatically different, he was however patient and smart enough to wait for the right opportunity to get what he wanted. And when the time came, he knew he had to do it without alienating anyone in the process.

The sweet sound of opportunity

MORITA'S UNCLE HAD lived in Paris for several years studying painting. As a result his wealthy family was fascinated by the latest wonders from the West, which Akio got to experience first-hand from an early age. He took avidly to reading the stories of great industrialists like Henry Ford, and listened with amazement when his parents upgraded to a new phonograph from Victrola, the company that dominated the field immediately after Edison's exit. The Morita family's new 'Victor Orthophonic Victrola' produced what was then considered high-fidelity sound and cost the equivalent of about $12,000 in today's money – back then it equated to half the cost of a new Japanese car. But to young Akio, it was much more than a new source of music – it was an epiphany. When he played his mother's old classical records on their grand new Victrola machine, he was awestruck at the sonic enhancement it brought to the same old scratchy discs. From that day forward he became utterly obsessed with electrical systems and gadgets, constantly hanging out with a cousin who'd built a primitive tape recorder and spending so much time tinkering with circuitry that his schoolwork began to suffer.

Driven by his desire to pursue his electronic experimentation however, Morita buckled down and made sure he got the grades required to pursue further studies in technology. He then talked his parents into letting him study physics, instead of something more suited to the 'eldest son's burden' of taking on the family business, such as law or accountancy. After all, he assured them, it was good for business to learn about the latest science and technology, and he could return home in plenty of time to take on his family responsibilities. In truth however, a lifetime of producing sake and miso could not have been further from his mind.

Global events in the shape of World War II suddenly conspired to get in the young man's way. As a top-of-the-class physics student at Osaka Imperial University, rather than be drafted, Akio chose to sign up with the Imperial Japanese Navy to continue his studies.

Upon graduation in 1944, the young Lieutenant Morita became a member of a navy team researching future radar and weapons technologies, which was regularly updated on the enemy's latest work. As a result Morita knew much better than most of his countrymen just how far ahead US technology was of Japan's war machine, even though official propaganda said just the opposite. He and Masaru Ibuka, a brilliant older researcher who quickly became a firm friend, also gained extra information by tuning into military communications on the short-wave radios to which they had free access but were forbidden and unavailable to ordinary citizens.

Then, in August 1945, the entire ancient cosmology of Japanese society was irrevocably turned upside down within the space of one and a half seminal weeks. After the atomic bombs hit Hiroshima and Nagasaki and Japan's subsequent formal surrender to the United States, Emperor Hirohito, one of a long line of leaders with the supernatural right to rule, renounced his divinity and became earthly with a ceremonial role. The immortal leader for all time was suddenly just another citizen.

Equally dramatic social change quickly followed as the occupying American forces oversaw a total transformation of Japan's ancient feudal order. The *zaibatsu* system was disbanded and wealthy, landed families like the Moritas had their estates requisitioned and redistributed. Time-honoured companies were obliged to accept trade unions for the first time – something that, to many, smacked of nothing short of communism.

The 'serendipreneur'

ALMOST SERENDIPITOUSLY, THESE changes aligned perfectly with the founding phases of Morita's entrepreneurialism. To him, the bending of rules and regular black-market procurement were the first expression of what he later called his 'ronin' approach to business. A 'ronin' is a samurai who no longer serves a master. He's a free agent who, rather than being in the service of a great warlord and a family with a grand tradition and history, must instead make his own way in a world where allegiances and future objectives are mutable and unpredictable.

Since serving a lord was the traditional raison d'être for the samurai warrior, the word 'ronin' was a very deliberate and pointed choice by Akio Morita. It was his way of preparing for the very different Japan that – as he had grasped long before most of his countrymen – had arrived with the end of the war. His pride in and identification with the symbol of the ronin expressed a new, more qualified attitude to authority and servitude, and a new emphasis on self-motivation.

Morita's prescience and insight owed a great deal to his natural curiosity, analytical mind and remarkably cosmopolitan upbringing. But ironically it was his spell with the military that gave him privileged access to concrete evidence of the huge changes for which his nation was destined.

Akio saw one thing clearly in all this change and confusion: opportunity. In the course of his wartime research, he and Masaru Ibuka had glimpsed the state of the art in new recording and radio technology, and they were confident that they could improve upon it. Typically, Morita diligently laid the human groundwork that would enable him to realise his ambition in a conciliatory, communicative style. He convinced his younger brother, and then his parents, that the best thing for the family and its now downsized food business would be if the second son were to assume 'the oldest son's burden'. Perhaps by being set free, Akio might even find an all-new way to make the old family name even greater.

Humble beginnings

SO IN MAY 1946, with the family's approval, Morita and Ibuka founded the Tokyo Telecommunications Engineering Corporation. Their first location was the burnt-out shell of a department store, then in a purpose-built wooden barn outside town. The company and its 28 founding staff paid the bills by labouring on humble services and networks for the reconstruction effort, but meanwhile worked fervently at the longer-term goal of creating cutting-edge audio and electronic equipment. The short-term need to generate revenue led to the company's first product being an automatic rice cooker, which wasn't very successful and was soon dropped.

In the early days of the American occupation, materials were hard to come by and strict regulations on movements and expenditure complicated almost every part of the manufacturing process. But the ever-resourceful Morita was happy to 'misallocate' funds to feed his workers, or buy black-market fuel from GIs to keep his trucks moving. And the fact that he always delivered his commitments also meant he invariably managed to wriggle out of any trouble with the authorities.

The company's first big success was a gadget that could be clamped on to an old AM radio to enable it to receive short-wave signals, something that had been newly legalised by the occupying Americans. It was a great democratic gesture, but not one that Morita wanted to use as a blueprint for the future. The kind of company Morita envisaged was not one that would make bargain accessories for other people's electronics products. His dream was to forge a brand that would be known for its own greatly valued product innovations.

But first they had to come up with a brand name that would work globally and was less cumbersome and industrial than 'Tokyo Telecommunications Engineering Corporation'. In 1958 after much toing and froing on different possibilities, Morita and Ibuka settled on a new name that was a mix of '*sonus*', the Latin word for sound, and the English word 'sonny', which Morita thought had a friendly ring to it. From this marriage, 'Sony' was born.

Miniaturisation makes it big

MORITA AND IBUKA led a successful string of innovations born of their curiosity and adaptability, but they also stayed true to their founding focus – creating products that broke ground in sound and picture quality. Another constant was Morita's preoccupation with miniaturisation, which intersected perfectly with the evermore crowded living conditions Japanese urbanites had to endure after the war. By simply looking at the post-war lives of ordinary Japanese people, Morita was driven to build consumer products much smaller than anybody had ever thought about doing before.

Sony was the first company to incorporate new technologies like transistors into such devices. Soon, it began experimenting with them in its research into new TV technology and, by the mid-1960s, Sony made the most critically acclaimed televisions in the world. The company's long partnership with Dutch electronics giant Philips led to the development of the CD in the 1970s – a decade that also saw the release of Morita's long-cherished idea of a truly personal music player, one he called the 'Walkman'.

Morita's simple, inalienable goal – making premium electronics products – enabled Sony to adapt and grow with every surprise and market development. And his personal flexibility, his willingness to see what the company needed from him as a leader, enabled him to nurture new talent and keep his company and its products so inventive and audacious for decades. Even as he had to leave behind hands-on innovation to deal with Sony's success, he had a unique gift for encouraging bold creativity to blossom in others.

creating a dignified company culture was a priority at Sony.

That was because, as much as he loved experimenting with electronics, Morita's greater goal was to build an organisation that would endure and have the tools to keep growing fruitfully. So when he realised early on quite how brilliant his partner Ibuka was at technological innovation, he handed over all responsibility for Sony's engineering to his old friend. Morita would miss tinkering himself, but it was a sacrifice he willingly made for the greater good of his company and his vision for it. By this time, Morita had started to understand that a lot more than great R&D and good financial management would be required to realise his dreams. He decided to focus on the broader issues, like marketing and distribution, that would help ensure that Sony's design and engineering got the attention it deserved.

Morita threw himself into his new role with typical vigour, showing an adaptive brilliance for every aspect of late-twentieth-century marketing and management. When the company's first 'pocket-sized' radio proved slightly too big for any real pockets, Morita had special shirts with ever-so-slightly oversized pockets made for his salesmen to wear on the job. Later, after he became important enough to start taking a company helicopter to plants and meetings, to get over the guilt of sitting in the passenger seat, Morita learned to fly himself, knowing he'd be useful if anything ever happened to the pilot.

From national icon to global force

MORITA OPENED SONY Centres – first in Tokyo, then on New York's Fifth Avenue and in other key cities – because he understood how much a premium image is enhanced by its own exclusive retail environment. He also recognised that the ability to expeditiously get new products into the customers' hands via its own stores would give Sony an advantage over established rivals and their strong distribution networks.

Morita's commitment to making Sony an international success still puts most modern frequent-flying CEOs to shame. In the 1960s he moved his family to the USA and made sure that they learned English. In September 1970,

Sony became the first Japanese firm to float on the New York Stock Exchange, which was followed a year later by a listing on the London Stock Exchange. Just as he'd had to venture back into unofficial markets to get the parts for his firm's first televisions, so Morita had to enter unfamiliar territory, both cultural and legal, in order to make Sony achieve his aspirations. In an era of punitive import/export regulations and taxes and widespread protectionism, Morita tirelessly charmed, wined and dined influencers, politicos, heads of state and royalty to win his company competitive terms and awareness as he set up outposts around the world.

It wasn't that the 'ronin' Morita lacked respect for established protocols; it was simply that to boldly go where no Japanese company had yet, he had no choice but to establish a new set of conventions that were entirely of his own making. Indeed, Morita's basic, innate decency – those ancient Japanese values of respect and paternal concern inculcated by his family – were vital precisely because so much else was so new and unprecedented. Civility and thoughtfulness was a vital counterpoint to all of Morita's audacious expansion – and this was surely a key part of why Sony's early success on American soil was met with none of the bad feeling that was later to be directed against Japanese car companies in the 1980s.

Creating a loyal and dignified company culture was also a priority at Sony. As the eldest son, Akio had always been warned that a good boss should never be *bossy*, and that it's a leader's job to show and prove to the team that their personal well-being and that of their company are one and the same.

All work and almost no PlayStation

THE LAST TRULY revolutionary product Sony launched was released in Japan in 1994, just a few days after Morita, following a stroke, had stepped down as chairman. The project, called 'PlayStation', had started off as a hardware collaboration with veteran videogame brand Nintendo, who wanted to move their games from expensive cartridges to CD-ROMs, but needed an expert technology partner to make the transition. When the two companies cancelled the joint venture, one rogue engineer, Ken Kutaragi, had resolutely continued the work in secret with the aim of making a standalone videogame machine. It was only the open-mindedness of Morita's deputy and successor, Norio Ohga, that earned Kutaragi a green light instead of a pink slip when his ronin ways with the PlayStation were discovered. Fittingly, Morita had first invited Ohga to join the company when the young engineering student had made a lasting impression on the founder with his strident but insightful criticism of a flawed early Sony tape recorder.

The PlayStation would become the most important commercial counterweight to Sony's general decline in the two decades since Morita's retirement. Sadly, in other fields where it was once seen as a visionary pioneer, like television, audio and telephony, Sony is now often perceived as just another company, despite its engineering and design prowess in many of these spheres. It's exactly the kind of convention-bound status Morita worked so hard to avoid.

Speaking at a relaxed conference panel in 2007, Steve Jobs said the reason it took an Apple to create the iPod was simply that, 'Sony wasn't able to develop the software' that would translate already-established digital technologies into a sexy, 'must-have' consumer electronics device. Jobs also believed Sony's organisational structure was too complex to enable it to create an iPod (we'll look further at how Jobs believed a company structure should be in Chapter Four).

Sony's failure to dominate the portable MP3 player sector in the way it had with the cassette-playing Walkman and MiniDisc wasn't simply a matter of ability. Sony certainly had the talent and the resources; what it lacked was the will to create something as intuitive and audacious. That was partly because of its stake in existing technologies, but also, ironically, because of Morita's foresight about the need to establish an ecosystem of hardware and software.

Morita acquired CBS Records in 1987 and Columbia Pictures in 1989 because he foresaw a future in which success in consumer technology could only be sustained with the right media to play on it. (In other words, that software sells hardware.) But trying to be all things to all people and becoming a content creator as well as a hardware manufacturer brought new problems of its own. Fearful of their new prized assets being rendered valueless by the advent of digital duplication, Sony created products with evermore complicated and intricate software and evermore complex copyright protection. In the process, however, the company managed to alienate some of its most ardent fans and, at the same time, left the market wide open for more democratic and revolutionary solutions.

Steve Jobs:

The Humaniser

IN 1967, LEWIS Mumford published the first part of his two-volume work *The Myth of the Machine*. In the book, Mumford, a celebrated writer, historian and philosopher, turned a critical eye on the technological revolutions that he had once celebrated as marks of human achievement and imagination.

In the twentieth-century western world, Mumford argued, the word 'technology' had come to designate too narrow and limited a set of methods and mechanical concepts. 'Technology', he said, had become synonymous with production lines and impersonal machines, with the impersonal logic of production and consumption and the eking out of financial efficiencies.

This was a problem, Mumford believed, because the origins of the concept of 'technology' were about so much more than the calculus of production and profit. Historically, Mumford argued, important technologies had always served the human, and not the other way round. Our tools were less important than our rituals, our social relations and the symbolic sounds and marks that made up our languages.

Mumford pointed out that the ancient Greeks, who had invented the concept of *techne*, applied it to any product of practical human endeavour – any art, craft or tool-making process by which humans imposed their imaginative powers on the physical world. Mumford believed that people had been progressively more inclined to miss out on this bigger picture since the Industrial Revolution. That the closed, glacial systems of modern technology marked a break with the idea's fundamentally human origins, and threatened to make us prisoners of the abstract systems of our own inventions.

The year 1967 was important for American technology in other ways. Not least because it was the year in which the Jobs family moved across the San Francisco Bay Area to the city of Los Altos. The family had made the move in the hope of securing a brighter future for their unconventional, smart and headstrong 12-year-old son, Steve. Steve was so bored at the Mountain View schools he'd attended up until that point that he threatened to drop out of education altogether if they couldn't find him a more suitable one.

The move to Los Altos put the family within the catchment area of the superior education district of Cupertino. It didn't solve all of Steve's issues with school, but it certainly helped address them. It also brought him into the proximity of the engineer Steve Wozniak, and companies such as Hewlett-Packard, where he would get his first summer job the following year. Where he'd once felt constrained and patronised by the technocratic production line of education, he now began to see new horizons and opportunities.

There's no suggestion that schoolboy Steve read Mumford's hefty tomes, but somehow his education, inside and outside the classroom, began to inculcate in him a similar sensibility to Mumford's. Steve loved technology too much to limit his understanding of it.

As he explained many years later:

> It's in Apple's DNA that technology alone is not enough … it's technology married with the humanities that yields us the result that makes our hearts sing. The reason Apple resonates with people is that there's a deep current of humanity in our innovation.

'Humanity' is perhaps not the kind of word you might normally associate with the most successful enterprise in global corporate history. But for all his technical virtuosity, Jobs was never a pure engineer, obsessed with the glacial symmetry and mathematical purity of his constructions. He was able to be so relentless, so passionate, so outspoken and so far-sighted, because he found a way to do a job that not only engaged his mind but also allowed him to put his heart and soul into everything he did. If you're going to give your all to your work, you have to find a way to work that accommodates your entire complicated, contradictory humanity.

The ineffable, unquantifiable mysteries of human existence informed his dreams and decisions as much as any hard numerical evidence – in that sense he was in accord with Marshall McLuhan, who said in a 1969 interview that 'Mysticism is just tomorrow's science dreamed today'.

That's why Jobs famously went on spiritual pilgrimages in his teens. It's why he stuck around to attend calligraphy classes after he dropped out of college; he said calligraphy was: 'beautiful, historical, artistically subtle in a way that science can't capture, and I found it fascinating.' The clarity and precision provided by science and engineering were vital concerns and lifelong obsessions for Jobs, but they were never enough.

It's astonishing how often, even today, this aspect of Jobs' achievement is ignored. People rightly credit Apple with proving to other businesses that aesthetics are absolutely fundamental to connecting with a technological product, rather than an afterthought or a luxury. 'The main thing in our design is that we have to make things intuitively obvious,' he said.

The approach that Steve Jobs had towards aesthetics – that a focus on design and 'user experience' could, if taken seriously, enable universal appeal – is a characteristic that continues to differentiate the company he created. No other organisation has so comprehensively married art and industry, humanity and technology, to seamlessly 'join the dots' across all aspects of its business with such a consistent language of appearance, functionality and style. It's how the company manages to seem aspirational for all of us, without excluding any of us. It speaks Human.

no other organisation has so comprehensively married art and industry, humanity and technology, to seamlessly 'join the dots' across all aspects of its business

An artist, an engineer and an entrepreneur, Steve Jobs understood our senses. He had not just good but superior taste that was inescapably attractive because it was articulated in a way that was not elitist but easy, intuitive, imaginative and accessible.

Computing. Smartphones. Tablets. Music. Movies. Animation. Publishing. Retail. These are all industries that have been revolutionised by Steve Jobs's contribution, and all 'sectors' that he enhanced by refusing to section them off from other aspects of human experience. As we've seen, this capacity to cut through the dryly technical to shared human values was evident from the earliest days of Apple. Jobs's passionate emotions and his engineer's intellect was what made him such a revered legend while he was still in his twenties. He was always deeply in touch with his own humanity.

However, as this second chapter of *Limitless* argues, you can only create a lasting revolution through business if you work out how to forge a shared connection that will enable you to bring other people with you, by free choice rather than force or fear. In the last decade of his life, when he also became the most revered corporate leader of our times, Jobs learned how to better listen to and accommodate the human needs, dreams and insights of the people around him too. It was perhaps only because of events that severely shook his sense of destiny that he ultimately ensured he delivered on his potential. The 12 years Jobs involuntarily spent away from Apple in the 1980s and 1990s are rarely explored, but they were pivotal to the success he and his company enjoyed once he came back. In 1995, two years before he returned to lead Apple, he said:

> I'm convinced that about half of what separates the successful entrepreneurs from the non-successful ones is pure perseverance … Unless you have a lot of passion about this, you're not going to survive. You're going to give it up. So you've got to have an idea, or a problem or a wrong that you want to right that you're passionate about otherwise you're not going to have the perseverance to stick it through. I think that's half the battle right there.

Steve Jobs had no shortage of perseverance. 'You don't skate to where the puck is; you skate to where it's going to be,' he would often tell his employees. But during his exile from Apple between 1985 to 1997 he effectively went from being an Edison-like inventor to a nurturer of cultures. He was still relentlessly obsessed in the service of his work, his company and its people but his expanded sensibilities and empathy transformed him into an altogether more complete and effective leader. That change heralded perhaps the greatest comeback story of all time.

The hero's journey

ED CATMULL, WHO is now president of Walt Disney and Pixar Animation Studios, knew and worked with Jobs for over 26 years. During a 2012 session at the *Wall Street Journal's* digital business conference, Catmull said he saw the Apple founder undergo many phases of personal development over that time:

> In the first phase, when he had a sort of reputation, I think people misunderstood [Jobs] and what he was trying to do. What I found was that over that time he was learning from those mistakes. That the way he negotiated, the way he interacted with people, initially didn't work very well, but he was so incredibly smart that he changed his behaviour. And a lot of people didn't get this or didn't see a lot of this [side of him], but the Steve that I knew for the last several years was very kind, he was very empathetic with people. And when he negotiated – as I saw him do with Disney – there was a notion of fairness and partnership which was very strong. Those things weren't there earlier.

Watching 50-year-old Disney movies with his young daughter, Jobs said, made him want to create something that lasted in the way they had endured since *he* was a child.

At Pixar, Steve Jobs trusted in the brilliance of Ed Catmull and John Lasseter. He stayed out of the story meetings headed by Andrew Stanton, because he wasn't so presumptuous as to think he had more relevant skill and expertise than their crack team. He'd ask Pixar staff for advice – like whether the studio's films should be transferred to DVD in pan-and-scan or stay true to their cinema ratio with widescreen – and then became a staunch advocate for their opinions in his meetings with Disney.

The house that Steve built

THAT WAS WHERE Jobs did get thoroughly involved: making things happen. He learned to make deals Hollywood-style, and secured $26 million from Disney to fund a debut feature. Pixar was floated on the stock exchange 10 days after the release of the resulting film, *Toy Story*. And with its belief in the future of computer-generated feature films having been emphatically rubber-stamped at the box office, Pixar soon moved into a spectacular new purpose-built headquarters, designed by Jobs, where it would soon build a reputation as the dream factory of the digital age.

In 1999, with a brief that would stand the test of time, Jobs instructed the architects to help realise his vision for a marvellous campus that 'had to look good 100 years from now'. The architects' relationship with Steve would endure, as they would go on to design many of Apple's stores, including the iconic glass-cubed Fifth Avenue flagship in New York.

Speaking about the common gathering area that brings together people from different disciplines and was literally and metaphorically the heart of his new headquarters, Jobs commented:

> If a building doesn't encourage collaboration, you'll lose a lot of innovation and the magic that's sparked by serendipity. So we designed the building to make people get out of their offices and mingle in the central atrium with people they might not otherwise see.

Within a year of *Toy Story*'s release, Jobs was starting to get back in the loop at Apple, where in his absence fortunes had declined and product ranges had sprawled aimlessly. When Jobs returned to the company in 1997, Apple bought NeXT and its state-of-the-art software, which was immediately retooled to replace the creaking Macintosh Operating System and formed the foundation of the future that would be crucial to Apple's comeback.

In addition to a new iMac, Steve revitalised Apple by combining his passions of music and technology to launch the iPod. He said:

> It's not about pop-culture, and it's not about fooling people, and it's not about convincing people that they want some-

thing they don't. We figure out what we want. And I think we're pretty good at having the right discipline to think through whether a lot of people are going to want it too.

Maybe that's why he also said:

To me a brand is one simple thing … trust.

By the time of his return to Apple, Jobs had become a less top-down person, one who understood when principles stopped being helpful and started hindering progress. His lessons in budgeting, streamlining and rethinking, learned over hard, lean years at NeXT and Pixar, fed into the clear, unfussy structure he established at the company after his return to the role of CEO. He had a clear, new vision.

'When Steve attacks a problem,' Adobe co-founder John Warnock memorably said, 'he attacks it with a vengeance.' That fact never changed. What did, however, was Jobs's understanding of what makes a revolution last, and his ability to grasp what the real problems and obstacles to Apple's success were. He realised that, to endure, you have to put as much effort into making friends as you do into overcoming enemies. The nicer guy really did finish first. And that's the thing about real business revolutionaries: they never stop surprising you, even well after their own times.

Pixar's headquarters is still celebrated as a cathedral of design excellence and creativity. It had its genesis with the immense empathy and understanding stemming from the two worlds of moviemaking and software coding that it was conceived to unite. Paying tribute to the legacy of its co-founder's lasting contribution, in 2012 Pixar named their home 'The Steve Jobs Building'.

You can only change the world if people want to follow

'THE SOURBALL OF every revolution,' wrote the American artist Mierle Laderman Ukeles in her famous 1969 essay 'Manifesto for Maintenance Art', is: 'after the revolution, who's going to pick up the garbage on Monday morning?'

Ukeles's manifesto was written after the birth of her first child and the endless list of domestic duties she was faced with after its arrival. Looking after a young child and a home made her reconsider her assumptions about art and achievement, and our celebration of the 'revolutionary'. She argued that the classic motivations of political 'revolutionaries' all represented 'The Death Instinct: separation; individuality ... to follow one's own path to death – do your own thing; dynamic change'. But, she wrote, actually living life from day to day was always also about 'The Life Instinct: unification ... the perpetuation and MAINTENANCE of the species; survival systems and operations; equilibrium'.

big ideas come unstuck when the little things are forgotten.

In other words, revolutions don't make a meaningful and sustained difference unless their leaders can see past their ideologies and their enemies to understand the realities of daily life for the people they claim to represent. Without that connection, one of two things will happen. The first possibility is that would-be revolutionary leaders will fail to see the change they envisage and fight for it through into the long term (a charge many historians level at even that ultimate revolutionary leader, Napoleon). The second is that – as stories from Orwell's fable *Animal Farm* to Visconti's movie masterpiece *The Leopard* also remind us – once the leaders take power, they become all the things they once fought to overturn.

find the right way to communicate the excitement of the future you can see, and others may well sign up to join the adventure.

In today's digitally enabled business environment, 'disruption' is widely celebrated as the ultimate expression of dynamic change – of revolutionary progress – in a particular sector. But businesspeople want to stick around to see the change they create really take root in the culture. Founders who don't want to sell off their disruptive start-ups as soon as their valuations hit some giddying number have to master the maintenance and equilibrium of the other half of the equation too. Creative destruction is all very well, but to benefit from it in the long term, you have to make sure that what you create is an improvement on what you helped destroy.

starting a radical business may depend upon an exceptional capacity to envision a different way of doing things, but to sustain one over time rests upon the ability to explain that vision to everybody else, and having the humility to adapt it to the ways 'ordinary' people live their everyday lives in a changing world.

When the upstarts of today become the big businesses of tomorrow, their capacity to remain relevant and revolutionary over the long haul will depend on their ability to remember, respect and never take for granted. Big ideas come unstuck when the little things are forgotten.

You have to maintain your systems and operations and attend closely to the needs, desires and expertise of the people around you. To sustain a business revolution after an initial success or innovation, you have to guard against lapsing into the same bad habits and age-old dangers – complacency, entitlement, arrogance and greed – that brought down the old elites after their own initial successes. Making change is one thing. Making a meaningful difference is something else altogether.

Starting a radical business may depend upon an exceptional capacity to envision a different way of doing things, but to sustain one over time rests upon the ability to explain that vision to everybody else, and having the humility to adapt it to the ways 'ordinary' people live their everyday lives in a changing world.

in other words, revolutions don't make a meaningful and sustained difference unless their leaders can see past their ideologies and their enemies to understand the realities of daily life for the people they claim to represent.

To think like a revolutionary, yet never act like a tyrant, over a long and productive reign, you have to channel your brilliance without believing it makes you better than everybody else. It's a fine balance and an unending education. There's always the danger that being too thoughtful can constrain your capacity to speak frankly or to entertain possibilities others won't see. Conversely, dictators never get to hear the wisdom of the people they boss around. Find the right way to communicate the excitement of the future you can see, and others may well sign up to join the adventure.

Simplify

Why great achievements

are built on daily routines

and simple disciplines.

How Humble Rituals Create Extraordinary Triumphs

IN THEIR DRIVE to cut through the relentless distractions and diversions of modern life, some businesses are prone to treating 'simplicity' and 'convenience' as two words for a single objective.

It's a common contemporary conflation, and thus an understandable oversight. But it's also a real pity. 'Convenience' – that word that entered consumer culture after World War II via bland pre-cooked processed meals and supposedly 'disposable' plastic goods – is a philosophy that prizes ease of use and consumption above all else, for both company and customer. 'Simplicity', on the other hand, means something less reductive.

The game of 'convenience' is about how much of the essence of a product – flavour, texture, aroma – you can get away with removing in order to make something easier to use and store. The art of simplification is about how to distil an idea to its essence without diluting or compromising its greatest qualities. The simpler you can make a design, the more potential and possibilities open up for the people who use it.

Like many first-time visitors, I first found myself pondering this distinction on an early visit to Tokyo. Things in Japan's biggest city seemed not only abundantly functional and accessible but also *thoughtful*. It's impossible not to cast an admiring glance to the details – for example, the way carefully textured ground surface indicators assist pedestrians who are either blind or visually impaired – that have been designed with such consideration for the people who use them and the environment in which they are placed. Nothing had been deemed too trivial to care about, and the experience of interacting with such an environment is always an emotional and humbling one.

In this chapter we will learn from those who embody the Japanese spirit of *shokunin*, the ethos of accomplishment grounded in the power of habit and patience.

the companies that value focus over clutter and restraint over symbolic grandeur are invariably the ones that go on to reap the rewards of their discipline over time.

This drive to simplify, pursued with conviction, is not just a design approach or a production philosophy, or even just an art. It's a genuinely spiritual sensibility, one that trusts in the patient devotion to the simple and unfussy as the most dependable route to spectacular and unimaginable feats.

This is why, at its most transformative, the urge to uncomplicate a business is always about something more than business alone. If you attempt to simplify solely because you think simplifying will be more profitable, the likelihood is that you'll end up unnecessarily complicating your offering.

the art of simplification is about how to distil an idea to its essence without diluting or compromising its greatest qualities.

As the stories that follow demonstrate, those who profit most from their simple ideas tend to be those who fundamentally believe in simplification, not just as an expedient or economic strategy but as a defining aspect of their identity. That's true for long-lived, world-renowned, best-in-class organisations such as Lego and Chanel but it's also true of those who lead by example, who inspire others by their unstinting devotion to their daily tasks and their unflagging respect for the materials they work with. Rather than creating cults of personality, such simplicity-obsessed figures – be they humble craftspeople, high-end technology experts or space travellers – make the case for the spirit of simplification by showing what sophisticated achievements can be made possible. It's precisely *because* simplification brings its own satisfactions to devout practitioners of paring down that so many other, grander benefits follow in its wake.

The companies that value focus over clutter and restraint over symbolic grandeur are invariably the ones that go on to reap the rewards of their discipline over time. It can be difficult to keep faith in simple virtues, or to keep a cool craftsman's focus, when living in a time in which information moves so quickly. That's where the spiritual side, the true faith that simplicity will win out in the end, is so important. You have to be able to dispassionately assess what really matters, then passionately pursue that end, ignoring every distraction along the way.

the ethos of accomplishment grounded in the power of habit and patience.

Simplification should not merely be a goal – something you can reach, then tick off your to-do list. The quest to simplify, when it's sincere, doesn't end there, or anywhere. If your drive to simplify is to be a path to business greatness, it has to keep informing everything you do.

Shokunin:

Simplicity as Habit

EVERYONE WHO LIKES reading about the habits of success-ful people – and there are a lot of them, given that the late Stephen Covey's book on the subject has sold over 25 million copies – clearly hopes that some small bit of what they read will somehow rub off on them.

Deep down, though, we all know that the secret of long-term success is not so much about any particular habit, but more about the value of habits at large. Provided they don't become mindless, joyless or automatic, habits – also known as routines and rituals – can keep us alert and on track in a uniquely worthwhile way.

It's not to mythical supermen that we should look for inspiration if we want to compete and excel at the trials we take on; it's to those circumscribed, disciplined pursuits that breed long-term excellence and expansiveness by insisting on unflinching focus on a very simple, and perhaps highly repetitive, task.

In Japan they have a word for those people who have the highest dedication to the beauty of the small task, the task that is repeated countless times, but never simply duplicated or unthinkingly automated. That word is *shokunin*.

No brand, no problem

'*Shokunin*' WAS THE word Kenya Hara, art director of Japan's 'no brand' retailer Muji, chose when the *New York Times* asked him to explain why so many visiting westerners are drawn to the everyday design ethos of Japan. In Japan, the *Times* noted, foreigners often feel that every little thing – not just the big, marquee design projects – appears to have been patiently considered, and lovingly refined, so that it works as well as it possibly can. It's not about grand design statements, but tiny, thoughtful human touches.

dedication and unwavering discipline, is the epitome of leadership by example, rather than instruction.

Hara is a prolific writer on design, as well as a professor at Tokyo's Musashino Art University, and was an avid disciple of simplification even before he joined Muji, a brand that shares his drive to simplify. In 2000, Hara curated an influential Tokyo exhibition, 'Re-design: Daily Products of the 21st Century', that paid tribute to everyday craftsmanship. Soon after that, he began consulting for Muji, and a year later was appointed as the company's art director.

Muji had been founded in 1980, with a promise of good value, 'no-brand' wares for the Japanese consumer. It was a different philosophy from the plainly packaged, generic, 'no frills' budget grocery product boom witnessed in the UK's supermarkets at the same time, because the low prices at which those stores offered their own 'no-brand' range were reflected in those lines' intentionally grim packaging. If you bought a supermarket's own no-frills cornflakes, 'cheap' was not only what your purchase was but it was also what its packaging screamed about you to your fellow shoppers through the mesh of your basket or trolley.

Masaaki Kanai, president of Muji, says:

> Muji was founded in Japan in 1980 as an antitheses to the habits of consumer society at that time. On the one hand, foreign-made luxury brands were gaining popularity within an economic environment of ever-rising prosperity. On the other, poor-quality, low-priced goods were appearing on the market and had a polarising effect on consumption patterns. Muji was conceived as a critique of this prevailing condition, with the purpose of restoring a vision of products that are actually useful for the customer and maintain an ideal of the proper balance between living and the objects that make it possible. The concept was born of the intersection of two distinct stances: no brand (*mujirushi*) and the value of good items (*ryohin*).

Providing a contrary, and inspiring, explanation for its minimalist aesthetic, he adds:

> Muji's concept of emphasising the intrinsic appeal of an object through rationalisation and meticulous elimination of excess is closely connected to the traditionally Japanese aesthetic of '*su*' – meaning plain or unadorned – the idea that simplicity is not merely modest or frugal but could possibly be more appealing than luxury.

Muji first launched with just 40 products, but the way it packaged and promoted them was altogether different. Its thrifty 'no-brand' not only offered value, but also the promise of an elegant, anti-clutter approach to design and retail. Muji's 'Lower priced for a reason' products flattered customers' sense of their own taste and refinement and 'make users feel the beauty and pride in living a simple and modest life'. When you shopped there, you were making a statement about your ability to buy for design values, rather than mindlessly following brand labels.

It was a brilliant strategy, because it made 'no-brand' an aspirational idea in itself. But, as subsequent events would demonstrate, it went much deeper than that.

I made my first visit to Japan for the 2002 FIFA World Cup, fell in love, and have been back every year since, including the year of the Tōhoku earthquake and tsunami in March 2011. The post-Fukushima shutdown of Japan's nuclear energy plants led to the generation of much less electricity, which meant that, for months, citizens and companies in huge areas of the country had to make do with minimal power.

It was a real privilege to get to see how people responded. Rather than bemoan their bad fortune, businesses and individuals did a lot of soul-searching about the consumer demands made and waste created. People adapted with typical Japanese grace and selflessness to the everyday reality of timed power supplies, metered blackouts and even, for some, the rationing-like unavailability of the most basic of goods.

Which brings us back to Muji, whose own response to the cultural fallout of Fukushima was impressive. The company announced its intention to use 20 per cent less power, packaging and materials in all its products in the future. Today, the company is systematically trying to re-engineer its products to make them even more sustainable, even more efficient to transport and even less wastefully packaged. Much of this innovation is fitting of not only to Muji's three-decade-old ideals, but also to the centuries-old concept of the *shokunin*. As Kenya Hara explained in the *New York Times* interview:

> A central aesthetic principle in Japan is simplicity, but it is different from simplicity in the West. Let me explain the difference by comparing cooking knives. For example, the knives made by the German company Henckels are well-crafted and easy to use because they are highly ergonomic.

The thumb automatically finds its place when you grab the knife.

Japanese cooks who have special skills prefer knives without any ergonomic shape. A flat handle is not seen as raw or poorly crafted. On the contrary, its perfect plainness is meant to say, 'You can use me whichever way suits your skills.' The Japanese knife adapts to the cook's skill (not to the cook's thumb). This is, in a nutshell, Japanese simplicity.

In 2012, American film-maker Jesse Flower-Ambroch also took inspiration from that tradition. His short documentary *Shokunin* followed Japanese-born master knife-sharpener Chiharu Sigai in his New York workshop, servicing painfully sharp and pricey Japanese knives like those to which Hara had paid tribute. In Flower-Ambroch's film, Sigai explains, 'The knives are all handmade, so even though they come from the same brand, they are all different. So one must look at them individually, then go about fixing them differently.'

Simplicity as sophistication

BUT JUST AS the *shokunin* spirit isn't restricted to ancient crafts, so its commitment to simplicity isn't only applicable to simple kinds of work and organisation. It's acutely relevant to those tasks and organisations we think of as brain-fryingly complex too. The *shokunin* spirit is Limitless in its possible outcomes precisely because it's about maintaining and refining the best possible practices for achieving everyday excellence. Today, that can make it a crucial guide for disentangling and giving direction in twenty-first century, hi-tech jobs that, by definition and necessity, are incredibly intricate in every way.

the secret of long-term success is not so much about any particular habit, but more about the value of habits at large.

Alex Hutton has been a prominent figure in the world of online security in the past few years, both as a senior staffer at firms such as Verizon and as a chair of investigations and industry-wide committees into data breaches, cloud security and other crucial issues for everybody doing digital business today. When he's not firefighting today's threats, Hutton's job involves understanding and predicting what kind of devilishly clever hacks and unimagined viruses businesses might have to ward off next. It's an understandably stressful role in a high-stakes field that, despite its potential financial rewards, has a high rate of staff burnout.

Hutton was inspired by a 2011 documentary celebrating the *shokunin* spirit, *Jiro Dreams of Sushi*. This captivating, feature-length hit celebrated the extraordinary lengths to which Jiro Ono, the 85-year-old chef, went to create incredible food for his restaurant. Although only a tiny, unflashy sushi bar in a Tokyo subway station, Jiro's restaurant has three Michelin stars and, though the expensive experience is no-frills and diners are in and out within an hour, there's a year-long waiting list all the same.

Jiro Dreams of Sushi celebrates the unflinching *shokunin* spirit that had seen Jiro Ono obsessively refine the same few classic dishes over several decades, just to create incomparable sushi. Over and over again, he put himself at great pains to create the perfect temperature, taste and unerring consistency in every piece of sushi that every customer was served.

it's not to mythical supermen that we should look for inspiration if we want to compete and excel at the trials we take on; it's to those circumscribed, disciplined pursuits that breed long-term excellence and expansiveness.

Alex Hutton was so inspired by Jiro's rigour and relentlessness that he decided to try to spread the *shokunin* spirit across the entire IT security community. On his blog, he explained how Jiro's dedication had affected *his* outlook, his sense of what it means to keep caring about every act you undertake, regardless of how often you undertake it:

As a security practitioner, as somebody who's responsible for risk management, how am I a craftsman? ... a possible cause [of burnout] might be a western-style expectation of recognition and self-worth and all these values, versus investing in what you do, the product you create, this concept of craftsmanship. And I realised those times when I've been most motivated at work, those times when I've produced the best work possible, when people have said to me, 'This is the best risk work I've ever seen', those were times when I've been on fire for the craft that I was creating, for the output that I delivered, and I really sweated every detail much like a craftsman would.

The further you want to get, and the more sophisticated the technology you use to get there – whether your work is in knife sharpening, or digital security, or a national space program – the more crucial it is that you master and respect the simple drills of everyday duty first.

In September 2012, Miles O'Brien, veteran space and science journalist and trained pilot, gave a speech at the Kennedy Space Center (KSC), to mark the fiftieth anniversary of the Merritt Island, Florida, facility. It was a bittersweet night, because thousands of jobs had been eliminated at the base in the previous couple of years. NASA's drastically downsized space programme had left the KSC – the place from where man had so dramatically blasted off from earth on 16 July 1969 to meet the moon – and it was now a mere shadow of its former glory. But

O'Brien's admiration for its people, whether departed or still on board, was undimmed. His words of tribute made explicit reference to the importance of dutifully respecting small, daily tasks if you want to achieve out-of-this world things. He said:

> The recurring theme here is of an extraordinarily passionate, proud, meticulous workforce that embraces a philosophy that is lost on many Americans. Here they take tremendous pride in everything they do – and for all the right reasons. The Japanese call this *shokunin kihitsu*. Literally translated: 'the craftsman's spirit'. But that doesn't do it justice.
>
> Those who ascribe to this way of life take pride in everything they do. In Japan, sushi chefs, fishermen, and carpenters all practice their craft – no matter how seemingly menial – with a driving sense of obligation to work to their utmost for the good of all.
>
> And here is an essential point: *shokunins* make something for the pure joy of it; carefully, beautifully, and to the best of their ability. It has nothing to do with fame or fortune. It is nothing short of an unyielding pursuit of perfection. At KSC, they have mastered a trade that demands it – and they have risen to meet the challenge time and again ...

it's not about grand design statements, but tiny, thoughtful human touches.

Perhaps one of the most incorruptible and admirable routes for inspiring people – or nations, or space programmes – towards any noble ideal is always practising what you preach. The *shokunin* spirit, with its insistence on dedication and unwavering discipline, is the epitome of leadership by example, rather than instruction. It's the antithesis of a cult of personality, because the *shokunin* spirit says charisma and self-projection are less important than dissolving your ego into your work. It's about getting things done, precisely, punctually and with unfaltering respect for and concentration on the task in hand. If you can sustain total devotion to and concentration on the essential core of the work you do and the materials you use, from fresh fish to iron, your quiet application can take your business to places others can't even imagine.

Lego:

The Click

IT'S CUSTOMARY TO begin stories of the rise and fall and rise of Lego with a brick: a headline about a brick, a fascinating fact about brick, a little story encapsulating the enduring power of the brick.

The brick is, of course, vital. The basic brick is the foundation on which the Lego legend was built. The brick, the single Lego brick, is what, in many cultures, people refer to as 'a Lego'. But at the moment when Lego really became Lego – *the* Lego, the twentieth-century toy brand that outlasted all the others – what was even more critical than the brick was the click.

Like the sound of one hand clapping, a single Lego block on its own is all but useless, unfit for its designated purpose of having fun (the name 'Lego' comes from the Danish words *'leg godt'*, meaning 'play well', and in Latin means 'I put together'). Get hold of a second brick, however, and suddenly things begin to click. According to Lego's statisticians, two two-by-four (eight-button) bricks render 24 possible shape combinations. Add a third brick and that number takes off to 1,060. Add three more and the Lego magic really kicks in: just six two-by-four bricks makes the lucky recipient into a near-billionaire of playtime possibility, with an incredible 915,103,765 combinations at their fingertips. The fine-tuned simplicity of the Lego brick is precisely what ensures the dizzying potential of its applications.

Whether they used mud, sand or mortar, humans have been making building blocks since the earliest civilisations. The real trick has always been getting the bricks to stick together and, after that, to remain stuck. Lego's most Limitless feat was creating a new kind of connection to address this need – a connection so simple and self-explanatory that any toddler can understand and master it.

Carpenter Ole Kirk Christiansen founded Lego in Billund, Denmark, in 1932. The company's early years had been marked by hardship and struggle, but coming through them had equipped the small firm with resilience and openness to innovation, both of which Christiansen knew would be vital for its long-term survival.

The company was also strongly devoted to the value of 'quality'. Godtfred Kirk Christiansen, the third son of Ole, who had worked with his father from the age of 12, always told the story of how he was helping out in the workshop one day when he decided to break with established protocol and not apply a third coat of varnish to the batch of toy wooden ducks he'd been finishing. He was sure that two coats of varnish would be plenty to make the toy as tough as it needed to be, and that he was setting an example that would save time and money in future.

But when Godtfred unveiled his money-saving innovation to his father, Ole was far from impressed. He may have thought it was taking the initiative, but that was meaningless if he didn't maintain the quality. Ole told his son to stay late at the factory so that he could apply the missing third coat of varnish and bring his sub-par work up to standard. The incident inspired a motto and a famous wooden plaque, commissioned by Godtfred, that preserved the words with which his father had chastised him: 'Only the best is good enough.'

Aware of the growing importance of plastic to the toy industry, Ole had the foresight to invest a substantial portion of Lego's hard-won early profits (from its high-quality, traditional wooden toys) in machines for the injection moulding of plastic.

Drawing unabashed inspiration from the existing sets of toy blocks that were already being produced, in various materials, by toy firms elsewhere in Europe, Lego's engineers spent several years attempting to develop the perfect iteration of the simple, ancient idea of the building toy.

The connection, the click – that crucial concept at the heart of Lego's success – only crystallised some years into the company's research and development process. On the long ferry trip back to Copenhagen from a major European toy fair in London, Ole's son Godtfred got talking to the chief toy buyer of a Danish department store.

Why, she asked him, did every Christmas need a new must-have toy craze to displace the last one? Wouldn't it be better if there were a type of toy that parents could add to with each birthday or Christmas present, rather than supplanting it? Wasn't there scope for a toy range that children could continue to expand, enhance and enjoy as they got older? Something that would grow along with them, instead of, as seemed to be the norm, being thrown away or gathering dust?

That question eventually turned into the simple, consumer-focused premise that became Lego's promise to every child on every box of Lego, however large or small: *everything* fits together.

Empire building

LEGO'S FIRST VERSION of rugged plastic blocks was launched in 1955. Industry experts were underwhelmed, but committed sales and distribution campaigns ensured reasonable, though less than spectacular, sales. It wasn't until January of 1958 that Lego completed and patented an improved block design that clicked together with ease and an audible snap. This was thanks to the addition of the little plugs on the back of each brick and sockets on their underside, which were moulded in a new thermoplastic called acrylonitrile butadiene styrene (ABS). Unlike the many other types of plastic with which the engineers had already experimented, ABS seemed to have just the right mix of toughness and flexibility to be the perfect material for Lego bricks. You could count on the new blocks sticking together for as long as you wanted them to, yet, wondrously, you'd also never have to struggle to pull them apart.

respect the click, and you can build anything you can imagine.

Over the 1960s and 1970s, Lego delivered on that idea of endless connectivity and limitless play, offering options to suit the imagination and dexterity of every child and the wallet of just about every parent. It became a primary-coloured fixture of childhood and a poster-product for the post-war wonder of plastic goods. It continued to elaborate on that original idea of connectivity for each new age, launching its electronic 'Technics' sets in the 1980s and its programmable digital 'Mindstorms' range in the early 2000s. Throughout all those developments, 'the click' remained the simple, unifying guarantee; however clever Lego became, any three-year-old could show that any piece of Lego would connect to any other piece of Lego.

Then came the theme parks, the stores, the cartoons and the videogames franchises. In fact, nobody had noticed that the company's procedures and objectives were in danger of becoming overly complex and mutually contradictory. And sure enough, by the late 1990s, Lego was established as a symbol of a new kind of retro-cool and playfulness. The generations who'd grown up with the toy in the 1970s had become magazine editors, music video directors and influencers of every sphere. They helped return the wonder-toy they had adored to the media spotlight. This suited the company's leadership, who welcomed what they considered long-overdue respect for its design philosophy and enjoyed the brand's newfound hipness. It reflected the company's long-held sense of itself back at itself. It also complemented what had by then become the management's stated focus: a dedication to 'brand building' through PR moves and coverage in taste-making magazines, rather than being preoccupied with the simple foundations and childlike pleasures that had always ensured the company's bottom line.

Cracks in the brickwork

BUT IGNORING THE bread-and-butter business of doing business soon led to where it always leads: looming trouble. New initiatives like expensive, limited-edition Lego sets based on great architectural landmarks may have won the hearts of the cognoscenti, but they hardly opened wallets in the way that Star Wars Lego, Harry Potter Lego and the like would do later.

In fact, by the time *Fortune* magazine and the British Association of Toy Retailers named Lego the toy of the twentieth century in the year 2000, the ominous threats to

Lego's survival in the next century were already becoming all too apparent to those inside and outside the business. Despite the sideshow of the media love-in and the plaudits for product innovation, the company was losing money every other financial year.

By 2004, Lego was losing almost a million dollars a day. The crisis had become so dire that CEO Kjeld Kirk Kristiansen – Ole's grandson and only the third leader of the business since it was founded – handed over the reins to an outsider for the first time in the company's 72-year history. Having been abruptly awakened to the fact that Lego's survival was at stake, Kirk asked a 36-year-old employee to replace him at the head of the family business in the hope of saving it.

Jørgen Vig Knudstorp had first stepped inside Lego's headquarters several years before that promotion, as a management consultant. Kjeld Kirk had been so impressed with his work that the 33-year-old consultant was then invited to join Lego on a full-time basis. Three years later, when he was asked to take over the entire business, Vig Knudstorp once again responded with speed and focus on the big problems facing the firm (rather than the fancy distractions at its edges).

A 'war room' was established, in which the new management team analysed the existing operations and pored over the numbers pertaining to every aspect of the company's business. The findings were jaw-dropping. In the name of being creative and new and living up to its eternal mottos of 'innovation' and 'quality', Lego's independent-minded engineers were by that time sourcing their various raw materials from no fewer than a thousand different suppliers. This piecemeal approach and the short-term, self-absorbed outlook of the creative teams behind it, had not only led to a byzantine ordering culture; it also meant that the company's impressive production facilities never ran at more than 70 per cent of capacity. Two-thirds of the 1,500 different plastic-part designs were no longer manufactured, even though they were still listed on the company's live product inventory. The Lego generals in the war room also noted that among those 1,500 parts, a core of just 20 per cent – i.e. 300 parts – made up the vast majority of all Lego sales.

The Fixer

FROM HIS TIME looking in as an outsider for hire, to his first days as an employee taken on to accelerate change in Lego's approach, Vig Knudstorp knew that what he had to contend with was a company culture that no longer functioned in a joined-up way. Lego's age-old selling point of simple, straightforward connectivity had ceased to apply to the organisation itself. Creative teams looked to 'innovation' and 'quality' as abstract, absolute goals, without cross-referencing them with the broader real-life concerns of the company and its finances.

The motto of quality-at-all-costs that had once been a great strength to the company had now become a weakness.

'This idea had become an emotional concept and an excuse to oppose new cost-saving initiatives,' Vig Knudstorp said. 'Any time there was something that someone didn't want to do, all they had to say was, "You cannot do that because of quality."'

The new CEO instituted all-new policies to encourage employees to think in the round. He also ensured that supply chains and distribution networks were radically simplified. Because the biggest-selling and most-used bricks had always come from a relatively small pool of designs, this had minimal impact on the end product, but ensured a significant reduction in the costs of getting there.

Where Lego had previously made ad-hoc purchases of materials for its products, Vig Knudstorp ensured that vital materials were secured in long-term fixed deals with suppliers so they were not subject to volatile market pricing.

In another break with the past, creative and financial teams were told to work together on product development from day one. Without compromising the product, this new emphasis of collaboration between fiscal and design departments hammered home Vig Knudstorp's message that a successful supply chain was the lifeblood of the business. His staff took this additional tenet to heart, and it soon became as important a part of the Lego philosophy – and as great a source of pride to its staff – as the founding watchwords of 'quality' and 'innovation'.

According to Vig Knudstorp, Lego's product development staff 'initially saw reducing complexity as pure pain'.

Over time, though, they understood that by simplifying the company's needs and unnecessary complexity, the new CEO had both honoured Lego's traditions and ensured that it would have a bright future. 'What they had seen at first as a new set of constraints could in fact enable them to become even more creative.' As a management consultant, he'd first arrived at Lego to see how its departmental bricks could be more efficiently rearranged; as the company's new leader, he helped them rediscover how to experiment and play in productive new ways. Vig Knudstorp simplified the culture and, with it, Lego's financial fortunes. As soon as the new CEO's policy of paring back kicked in, Lego boomed again. Today, it has embraced digital-printing technologies that have extended its range of designs and possibilities way beyond the peak numbers from its period of wasteful, piecemeal production. But today it's done it all with an efficiency and a keen shared understanding that the pleasure of making things is more satisfying and more likely to last if it happens in a sustainable, streamlined environment, as opposed to an ivory tower.

During the time that Jørgen Vig Knudstorp's plans for cultural change were being implemented at Lego, 'Only the best is good enough,' the message on the old wooden sign carved by Godtfred in honour of Ole, was superseded by words from a memo written by a twenty-first century manager. The note was stuck to the fridge door in a staff kitchen, and it read, 'The best cooks are not the ones who have all the ingredients in front of them. They're the ones who go into whatever kitchen and work with whatever they have.'

Thinking outside the toy box

BEYOND THE PHYSICAL bricks, Lego's refocused outlook has also helped its broader branding strategies become financial powerhouses, rather than the window dressing they once were. From the dozens of Lego-branded video-game bestsellers to *The Lego Movie,* the company is now thinking far beyond the toy box.

'Everything is Awesome', the title song of the 2014 Warner Bros. animated feature, could well be the soundtrack for the company as a whole in recent years, with its lyrics 'Everything is better when we stick together'. Like so many other recent innovations from the company, *The Lego Movie* was a gigantic box-office hit. And, while it unashamedly and uproariously tapped into all the childlike fun and invention associated with the beloved legendary toy, like all the best children's stories, it also had hidden philosophical depths behind the primary colours.

Like the physical bricks, the digitally animated *Lego Movie* advocates experimenting and inventing to find your own path. In one knowing scene, a child and an adult argue over what Lego is. 'It's a toy,' says the kid. 'No, it's a versatile interlocking brick system,' the grown-up replies. Either way, for the company and for the builders who love it, the recipe for staying relevant has always been returning devoutly to the studied, scrupulous simplicity of the click, and the phenomenal scope it offers to build new and better things.

Lego continues to cook up a profitable storm. Thanks to its alchemical ability to turning plastic that costs one dollar per kilo into toys that sell for close to a hundred times that amount, Lego's global revenues have seen it surpass Mattel (the home of Barbie, Hot Wheels and Fisher-Price) to become the world's number one toymaker.

It's surely no accident that Lego, the 'Toy of the twentieth century' that survived its era of dangerous over-complication to re-emerge as the toy of the twenty-first, is rooted in absolute simplicity. The objectives that saved Lego – the drive to pare down your product range to the components that actually matter, to keep seeking new efficiencies in what you do, to have a deep respect for your materials and vigilant eye on how they're supplied from you – are also those that made Ford's Model T the emblem of modern manufacturing. It's for much the same reasons that IKEA is the world's biggest and the best-value interiors company. When you know what you stand for, and when you attend to that practical core of your business with such vigilance and engagement, you have a foundation so solid that it frees you up for greater feats of imagination.

In a world where even children's play has become ever-more high tech (just look at the number of preschoolers now being babysat by an iPad) it's all the more impressive that something that's been around for more than 80 years is still flourishing. It's a testament to the potential and staying power of a simple idea, executed with absolute dedication. Indeed, the fact something as brilliantly low-tech as interlocking plastic bricks still rule the hearts and creative minds of so many of the world's children feels almost miraculous. At least until you remember the first rule those bricks teach anyone who picks them up: respect the click, and you can build anything you can imagine.

Chanel:

The Embodiment of Simplicity

FASHION ALWAYS LOVED Coco Chanel, but Coco Chanel didn't always love fashion. She said what she thought about her fellow designers, even when it wasn't good (which was often). She defied the logic of trends even though it was the fundamental principle of the fashion business. She all but left the industry when she closed down her global chain of boutiques in 1939, yet in 1954, when she reopened them, she went on to enjoy one of the greatest fashion comebacks of all time. Her reputation as an incomparable force and peerless pioneer in the history of fashion has never looked remotely at risk since.

Coco Chanel's resistance to 'fashion' was one of the keys to her eponymous company's success when she returned to the business in the 1950s, just as it had been in 1913 when she opened her first boutique in the Normandy beach resort of Deauville. Unlike every other fashion designer, Coco was never willing to reinvent the wheel every season just because the logic of the industry's calendar and media demanded it. Her vision was like a kind of luxury Lego: to offer women a wardrobe they could continue to expand

and embellish organically over the years, and to create a classic look that transcended what was 'in' or 'out' because it was rooted in the more enduring daily reality of the human body and its experience in the world.

Chanel's vision: her clarity of thought and her deep commitment to putting her artistry at the service of the women who wore her clothes, rather than making mannequins of them.

This touchstone enabled Chanel to devise innovations – from the fashion logo to the statement handbag – that soon became industry-standard ideas and crucial revenue streams for all fashion houses. Chanel's pursuit was of something altogether more singular than being anointed 'star of the season'. She didn't fit the rat race of fashion because she sought – and became uniquely associated with – the more permanent concept of *chic*.

Chanel owns 'chic' to this day because Coco Chanel believed a woman should wear her clothes, and not the other way round. Her design ethic was about quality and simplicity, about clothes that always stood out but never shouted for attention. Her unfussy attitude to fabrics and her perfectly pitched sense of style enabled her to reimagine fashion as something that could last. The little black dress, the 'interlocking Cs' Chanel emblem and Chanel No. 5, the world's best-known bottled scent – all now approaching their centenaries – are just three of the most obvious Chanel creations for which millions still give thanks every day.

Even by 1954, when Chanel unveiled her first new collection in 15 years, she had some old tricks up her sleeves that instantly took off – like the over-shoulder handbag, which she had invented in the 1920s but made over, to huge success, on her return. (The most recent time there was an 'it-bag' craze in high fashion, in the early 2000s, Chanel's old classics were once again pivotal to the revival.) Elsewhere, though, the philosophies of younger designers were hogging the headlines and gaining all the acclaim for their creativity. Just as the intricate and avant-garde designs of her 1920s rival Elsa Schiaparelli had led Chanel's critics to accuse her of being conservative and predictable, so a new wave of post-war European designers seemed to threaten to leave her behind with their flamboyant approaches.

In 1947, 'The New Look', with its sharply edged glamour, launched the name of Christian Dior, and in the years immediately following many other designers – almost all men – made their reputations by stretching the outline of women's fashion further still. The Spanish designer Cristóbal Balenciaga did women the favour of relaxing Dior's pinched, bombshell waistlines, but he also padded and extended the shoulders of his breakthrough designs. This made for a striking form, but if you were anywhere but on a catwalk it wasn't always functional. In fact, it was precisely the kind of cartoon-like extension and adornment of the female body, symptomatic of that generation of young, all-male designers, that seemed to be on Chanel's mind when, without naming any names, she launched one of her trademark attacks on 'fashion' in the 1950s, declaring:

> Fashion has become a joke. The designers have forgotten that there are women inside the dresses ... [Women] want to be admired. But they must also be able to move, to get into a car without bursting their seams! Clothes must have a natural shape.

That observation says a lot about Chanel's vision, about her clarity of thought and her deep commitment to putting her artistry at the service of the women who wore her clothes, rather than making mannequins of them. Of course, the bold male designers who had thrived in the industry in her absence could never actually *wear* the clothes they designed, but by the late 1950s the same could increasingly be said of the average woman. By that time, Yves Saint Laurent and André Courrèges (the inventor of the mini-skirt), were the latest design darlings of French fashion. They were brilliant young men who seemed to create their sculpted clothes with only the youngest, most lithe bodies in mind, and with comfort nowhere in their considerations. In their quest for spectacle and statement, the male fashion designers of the day seemed to be ever-more like puppetmasters, directing their female followers in their unforgiving outfits.

The difference between Chanel's classic chic and the approach of her rivals, whether in her first decade in business or her seventh, came down to this very straightforward difference. She wasn't dressing up someone else to embody an impossible fantasy. She was making clothes she could, and did wear, designing products not just to be aesthetically admired, but also to be useful – to be wearable, lasting, and to give a little bit of extra help and confidence to any woman trying to make her way in a world where men usually got to define the roles. But, at the same time, that eternal fashion essential, 'mystique', was always important. A reason she first became a sensation after her 1913 boutique opened was that she had taken a fabric used for underwear, cotton jersey, and retooled it as a comfortable, flexible material for thoroughly comfortable women's outerwear with couture-level finishing. She'd made an ordinary fabric into an aspirational one, turned intimate underthings inside-out and into the arena of high style 60 years before later designers shocked with their noisier takes on the same idea.

formal excellence is always admirable, but when it's combined with feeling, and done at the scale of the human rather than the monumental, it can become something much greater.

In an effusive 1931 *New Yorker* profile of Chanel, the magazine reminded its readers how radically practical Coco had been from the outset:

> The first iconoclastic simplification that Chanel made in the mode was a cobalt tricot sailor frock that might have been worn, at least in masquerade, by the French navy, and, in her twenty remarkable years since, she has brought the essential items of most of the other humbler trade costumes into fashionable circles ... The key to her peculiar genius and its sartorial consequences may lie in the fact that Chanel, most Parisian and expensive couturier of her epoch, was born poor and in the country.

With no airs and graces, no pretensions about 'high' or 'luxury' culture or fabrics, Chanel was able to focus on what it felt like to wear or see her style, and to cut through all the inherited pretensions and hierarchies around fabrics and fashions. She really did mean it when she said, 'Simplicity is the keynote of all true elegance.'

A cut above the rest

AN ERSTWHILE TOMBOY and lover of men in uniform, Coco Chanel had learned a great deal about the subtle power of detail by studying menswear. That's why you still associate her name with a certain length of skirt, a certain subtle height of heel and the flow of a lapel, with simple details that grant distinction, rather than slashed skirts or daring backless structures. It wasn't cowardice that led Chanel to avoid the kind of racy designs people sometimes call 'brave'; it was her belief that women had better things to do when they went out in the world than worry about a stray breeze embarrassing them or a silly heel sending them flying.

While headline-seeking young designers started to raise hemlines and slit dresses to expose the flesh beneath, Chanel's choices of cut and fabric rarely went beyond rarefied suggestion. She didn't see isolated exposure as any match for the full 'flow' of the whole woman in the right outfit:

> I wanted to give a woman comfortable clothes that would flow with her body. A woman is closest to being naked when she is well-dressed.

Chanel is justly celebrated for such enduring lines of her own, but she also read widely and had a wonderful assortment of amusing remarks from historical greats. However, while we have a good idea about her library and have a definite string of key dates – including the creation of Chanel No. 5 fragrance in 1921 and the creation of the Chanel symbol four years later – trying to get to the roots of Chanel's specific design inspirations is almost as impossible as working out the finer biographical details of her life. She told many versions of her life – all of them more glamorous and less painful than the reality: an absent father, years spent in an orphanage, the man she loved killed tragically while still young. Even the metamorphosis from her given name, Gabrielle, to 'Coco', is the subject of several diverse and colourful stories.

Furthermore, a creation as well known as the Chanel No. 5 fragrance – which, almost a century later, is arguably the most recognisable in the world – is shrouded in mystery. Its name might have been a religious reference learned from her time being raised by nuns after her mother's death. Or it may relate to the fortune teller who once told her that five was her lucky number. And as for the distinctive shape of its bottle, the most compelling tale is that it was a tribute to the flask in which Coco's one-time love, Arthur 'Boy' Capel, carried his whisky.

It's entirely fitting that the stories beyond the design classics that Chanel left behind will never be cleared up, any more than her life will. Trying to disentangle the threads would probably be to miss the point of her uniquely imaginative presence in the fast-moving history of fashion. Chanel fused the bold, stripped-down geometry of her modernist era with something more intimate and personal. She gave her designs to the world, but still managed to keep the secrets of how she'd triumphed as a woman in what was a man's world. And it was precisely by doing so that she was able to create such an enduring vision and such a durable brand. Formal excellence is always admirable, but when it's combined with feeling, and done at the scale of the human rather than the monumental, it can become something much greater.

Coco Chanel died at age 87 in 1971 at the Hotel Ritz in Paris, where she had resided for more than 30 years. With Coco gone, the fashion house she built endured a decade of personnel changes and false new starts until Karl Lagerfeld took charge in 1983. First as chief designer and today as creative director, Lagerfeld went back to Chanel's founding achievements (and the power of the logo she created) to re-energise the label's offerings. Along with Maureen Chiquet, the Chanel CEO since 2007, who has masterfully steered the brand in the modern age, he deserves the acclaim, but has generally refused to bask in it. Even today, the plate on the door of Lagerfeld's office at Chanel reads 'Mademoiselle'.

In September 2000, both Karl Lagerfeld and Yves Saint Laurent unveiled new collections that seemed to hark back to Coco Chanel's monochromatic elegance, with white blouses worn over black skirts in a way that was as strikingly effective as it was simple. After all those years of outdoing her unfussy blueprint for chic with extravagant designs, the designers who took her mantle seemed to be saying that, in the long run, nobody could ever eclipse her achievement. After his show, Karl Lagerfeld was asked if he was trying to take fashion back to the beachside town of Deauville, where Coco Chanel set up her first boutique. His answer? 'It never left.'

The Empire established by the mistress of chic, the queen of the stylishly simple, was sustained by sticking to Chanel's no-frills, all-thrills understanding of women and their wardrobes. It's only right to defer to Coco as 'Mademoiselle', as the visionary pioneer behind the business success of Chanel and scores of other twentieth-century fashion houses. But it's also true, however absurd it seems, that we can still trace that success to her unruffleable sense of the simplicity of her task. Coco Chanel really was, as she insisted to the last, 'just a simple little dressmaker'. Today's hottest and grandest designers could do worse than emulate that plain-sounding, customer-focused statement – especially if they still want to be on top tomorrow.

It all comes down to the essentials

ONLY A HANDFUL of human beings who have ever lived are in a position to testify that the power of simple, humble habits can take us into orbit. The Ontario-born astronaut Chris Hadfield is one of them. He's the man who headed to the International Space Station in late 2012 and, over his journey and the months in space that followed, became the most famous spaceman of the social-media age, posting multimillion-view video blogs and covering David Bowie's 'Space Oddity' in orbit. As such, he not only has the experience to say how unimaginable feats are built but he is also more than equipped with the eloquence to do that experience justice.

Speaking in his native Canada a year after his return to earth, Hadfield tied together simplicity and the *shokunin* habit with his interstellar achievement. He said what made the journey possible was years of daily drills. If you or I were plucked off the street and into the cockpit of a shuttle, with responsibility for several lives and control of a console with hundreds of switches, we'd rightly be terrified. But having trained for 15 years before the mission, Hadfield was thoroughly prepared:

They say, OK, you're preselected ... We're going to teach you so much about every single switch that you will know them more intimately than anything you've ever known in your life ... if you spend the years in advance ... it becomes more like beautiful music that you're part of and less like a daunting, scary, petrifying thing.

This respect for unglamorous routine, Hadfield argued, was the key to conquering fear and moving into new territory. Those drills, done so frequently and so attentively that they became second nature, enabled him to conquer fear, master his environment and realise the 'impossible and scary dreams' of space travel he'd first had at nine years old. The simple enabled the spectacular; practice made the impossible real; and his dutiful years as a student turned him into a leader, giving him what he termed 'a set of experiences and a level of inspiration for other people that never could have been possible otherwise'.

Just as astronauts know from direct experience that the simple is the route to the spectacular, so the stories of Coco, Lego and co. prove that the same is true of business. A toy brick may seem easy to approximate; a blend of scent or a cut of cloth sounds, in theory, something easy enough for rival firms to dissect and replicate. But in practice, these masters of simplicity have known their markets and materials so well that – though there have been many attempts over these businesses' long histories – nobody else has come close to rivalling the fundamental things they have done so well.

This principle holds today, even though our material world is augmented by evermore digital mediation and virtual commodities. In some respects, the complexity of the information age makes the drive to simplify more vital and visible than ever. We're all drawn to anything clear and useful enough to enhance our sense of control and enable our appetite for adventure in an over-accelerated world.

It's not just IT security experts and astronauts who prove this point. Consider the twenty-first-century technologies every one of us uses, and the way the most powerfully simple always make the greatest connections, often seeing their commercial values soar in the process. Today, many people's preferred social network is Instagram or Snapchat, which all but do away with words and, like emoji, return us to the pictographic origins of language. The earliest written languages were image-based scripts designed to enable commerce between far-flung peoples as efficiently as possible. The drive to simplify, pursued with dedication and unfaltering application, has a way of reminding us what really matters.

Gimmicks will never go away, in the digital world or any other, but for those modern businesses that want to become and remain the best in class for decades, mastering simplicity remains a wiser bet. If you can muster the patience and dedication to master your medium, the scope for building on that foundation, block by block, is vast.

Simplifying is less a goal than a kind of rhythm – a pulse you can come back to again, every time a project or a business seems overly complicated, too scrappy or stretched too thinly over too many diverse concerns. The impulse to simplify a discipline, when properly respected, should never become boring or seem irrelevant. The great simplifiers in business history never lost touch with that quiet truth. When everything seems too much, too convoluted, too intricate, paying proper attention to the little things that really matter can always pull you out of the confusion.

Organise

*Counterbalance creativity
and experimentation with
good systems and
operational excellence.*

Great Businesses *are* Never 'Built'
– *they* Remain Works *in* Progress

'ONE OF THESE days,' Robert De Niro says to Cybill Shepherd in *Taxi Driver*, 'I'm gonna get organizized.' De Niro's character, Travis Bickle, has noticed the phrase on a kooky office sign he's seen, and quotes it to try to lighten the mood on a disastrous first date. He thinks it's something she, and most people, will connect with: vowing to get one's life in order, while jokily misspelling the all-important word 'organised' in a way that suggests that actually doing it will remain a pipe dream.

This well-intentioned idea of 'getting organised' just as soon as you can get around to it is one that, like the average New Year's resolution, is usually destined to fail. Just like so many people do in their lives, workers at many companies view 'getting organised' at work as a clearing up the desk at the end of the year, or the ritual shuffling of departments with which a new boss inevitably makes a symbolic mark (or 'reorganisation') on the business. They're seen as processes that have to be endured before you can get back to what you're actually paid to do.

The most effective people don't treat organisation as a chore or an annual spring clean. They see it as the best way to start realising their goals now, instead of in some mythical 'then'.

businesses have developed from maverick start-ups into mature businesses, getting bigger without becoming bulky, scaling up without slowing down and nurturing creativity without endangering stability. When hard work is understood as part of the formula for happiness and fulfilment, when change is accepted and embraced, when thoughtful organisation is understood as the key to achievement, it's unwise to impose limits on what you might be able to do.

Leaders of the most effective companies think the same way, and make sure their staff understand and benefit from the fact that it's the best way too. They understand organisation as an hourly, daily and weekly challenge. They willingly embrace the responsibility of making the business function as effectively as it can, and they encourage and empower their workers to do the same.

When the people at a company understand its organisation as a pillar of the company's identity and success, and they feel a part of this, wonderful things happen. They repeatedly prove their ability to react swiftly in fast-changing business environments and to discover new markets before their rivals. Staff stop seeing organisation and creativity as opposing forces and embrace the fact that, for a business to excel, endure and fulfil its potential, those two forces must be understood as two parts of the same process. Creativity is great, but if you keep missing your deadlines and breaking your budgets, you won't get to enjoy it for long in a world of profit and loss.

If a company is to function as a cohesive, creative and responsive whole, if it is to grow and mature without losing the energy and imagination with which it started up, then the organisational ethos must be clearly communicated and sincerely signed up to by everybody who is a part of it.

As usual, phrases and formulas can only take us so far with this stuff. The precise nature of each great company's way of championing organisation – the form and tone in which the value of being organised is conveyed – depends on the type of business in consideration, and the kind of world in which it finds itself operating. Walt Disney, Pixar, Netflix and Nike built brilliant corporate cultures along very different lines for very different times and challenges. Because these businesses were so clear about why and what their fundamental goals were – providing family entertainment, in the case of Netflix, Pixar and Disney; enabling athletes, in the case of Nike; simply keeping alive and driven, in the case of Samsung – they were able to rethink, rebuild and adapt their organisations with a freedom and decisiveness that made them pioneers, over and over again. Being so singular about their ultimate objectives, these companies were free to boldly iterate and experiment about the best way of getting there. They all mastered the rare operational flexibility that empowered growth without hampering responsiveness, and that retained creativity without risking disaster.

Creativity, commitment to the cause and experimentation arise naturally in any worthwhile start-up – but these qualities don't always scale. Good systems and operations are a hallmark of many big and respected corporations, but they often go hand-in-hand with a box-checking boringness.

Whether as businesspeople or customers, we've all experienced companies where a 'computer says no' mentality prevails – businesses in which 'the system' by which the organisation operates is regarded, even by the staff who work in it, more as a hindrance than a help. Legacy systems that were originally conceived to make a business more efficient can encumber efforts and slow progress when times change. The very best organisations cultivate and perpetuate that enthusiasm for the new and the different by constantly adapting their administrative systems as they grow and change.

Ultimately, it's not the fireworks at the birth of a business that set the groundwork for long-term success; it's the way the company matures and copes with its teething troubles and growing pains.

Growing up the right way – creating new teams, recruits and financial backers that share and strengthen your vision, rather than threaten it – is a difficult and delicate task, and one that is never complete. It is like growing a houseplant: it requires constant watering, pruning and attention.

If you're pushing yourselves, you're going to face crises. If you want to employ great, smart, motivated people, and you want to keep them happy and productive, then you have to accept that they're going to have expectations of you too. Get the formula wrong, and you'll alienate the talented people that make your company special.

Organisation is a vital but incredibly hard thing to get right, and keep getting right. That's why this chapter is about the exceptional ways in which businesses have developed from maverick start-ups into mature businesses, getting bigger without becoming bulky, scaling up without slowing down and nurturing creativity without endangering stability.

When hard work is understood as part of the formula for happiness and fulfilment, when change is accepted and embraced, when thoughtful organisation is understood as the key to achievement, it's unwise to impose limits on what you might be able to do.

Disney's Circle of Life

TALKING ABOUT THINGS has many virtues, but one of its drawbacks is that it prevents you from getting on and actually doing them. That's why those rare organisations that achieve maximum internal communication and operational clarity with minimal verbiage are so often the very same ones who develop and deliver results most rapidly and efficiently too.

For that reason, I've long been fascinated by the organisational structure of one of the twentieth century's most recognisable brands, as documented in the years during which its founder, Walt Disney, had just overseen the now-classic films *Snow White and the Seven Dwarfs*, *Pinocchio*, *Dumbo*, *Fantasia* and *Bambi*. Every one of those films incorporated a raft of new ideas and equipment, yet every frame of each of them is an unfading work of art. They alchemised his name into the essence of an enduring modern mythology.

Disney conveyed the structure that spawned his early classics as a simple, single graphic showing how everybody at the company collaborated. Rather than using the standard visual logic of the familiar branching tree-style org chart, with its pyramid of little boxes layered in order of what can only be read as descending importance, the egalitarian Disney chart takes the form of a circle, with numerous connecting departments and divisions. Those divisions – 'sound', 'editing', 'paint & ink' and so forth – are all around, with the departments that report into them clustered close by. All these points ultimately connect into the studio's leadership, as represented by a smaller red circle, marked 'Direction', which is positioned in the centre. Instead of rigid tiers of management, where the leader's sensibility trickles down rank by rank, the circular organisation chart expresses an objective of absolute inter-connectedness.

As well as style, there's also an unlikely element of poignancy to this chart. It was drawn up in 1943, a year after the success of *Bambi*, and six years after the make-or-break release of *Snow White*. Because of Disney's plans to expand into areas such as theme parks, and the budget restrictions his company experienced following America's entry into World War II, he would never again be so inti-mately involved in his animated features. For many critics, that first sequence of five animated films remains the golden age, the high point of the form – even into this digital day.

The Disney Studio depicted in that organisation diagram has undergone countless evolutions in the 70-plus years since the illustration's first public appearance. The techniques by which the world's best animated films are produced today are different in almost every possible way, but their emotional and artistic ambitions are still informed by Disney's vision. Little wonder, then, that, even as a relic of another age, Disney's 1943 chart still manages to make the organisational charts of so many twenty-first century businesses look hierarchical, bureaucratic and utterly inflexible.

The Apple core

THE ORBITAL LOGIC of Disney's chart was always impressive, but it became more interesting still after the spring of 2011 when *Fortune* magazine published a graphic depicting the way Apple had been organised since Steve Jobs's return to the company. The *Fortune* chart took the form of a circle, with CEO Jobs at the centre, the names of the heads of the various teams – software, industrial design, retail, and so forth – arrayed all around and their direct reports, in turn, fanning out around them. All points led to or from the nucleus of Jobs at what can only be seen as the core of the Apple enterprise.

This pair of pictures, with their genetic kinship, says more than any number of words could. If the visual expression of Disney's brilliant leadership could remain so relevant all the way from Walt's day to Steve's, it's reasonable to wonder if it's a model that goes back beyond even the earliest days of Disney.

We know that, in his time with Pixar, Steve Jobs's style and philosophy became informed by his appreciation of Disney's enduring creative achievements. But what about *the cycle of growth and development – driven by the impossible, yet essential, pursuit of perfect organisational synchronicity and a holistic system – and the new challenges of each day were in perpetual motion.*

Walt? The Disney Studio's anti-angular organisational map, with its two-way feedback loops between departments, suggested an ongoing cycle, rather than a fixed and fossilised bureaucracy. Yet its housing within a circle – that ancient symbol of eternity – communicates a kind of wisdom and clarity that seems to touch on ideas much older than the 'Father of Animation'. Whether he knew it or not, Disney's org chart, and its system of problem-solving in concentric circles, bears an uncanny resemblance to an ancient symbol called the mandala.

The right circles

A MANDALA IS a pattern contained within a circle. It has a smaller circle at its centre representing the nexus of power, with various shapes, circuits and secondary figures from its wider cosmos arranged all around. Though no two mandalas are identical, all share a basic structuring principle.

In many cultures, mandalas have been seen as analogies for the human body and its intricate, diverse, but ultimately unified workings. This is perhaps understandable when you consider that the word 'organisation' has its roots in Greek, where it stemmed from the same term as 'organic', and meant 'the condition of being ordered as a living being'.

In other words, take away the particular titles and the culturally specific labels and symbols, and the organisational charts of Apple or Disney are mandalas for when those companies were at profound moments of creativity and productivity. Interestingly, it was in 1923 that the celebrated psychoanalyst Carl Jung first started studying mandalas and the cultural universality they seemed to possess. This was the same year that Walt Disney and brother Roy launched their own 'Disney Brothers Cartoon Studio'.

Like Disney's chart, Jung's interest in mandalas was a response to the challenges of the modern world. He used them less as guides for leading groups of people, and more as self-help exercises. Doodling his anxieties and ambitions within two circles, Jung felt able to engage with contradictions in his make-up and reconcile conflicting moods. He saw it as a way to unify the ever-changing concerns and competing aspects of the self. Jung was equally heartened when his researches demonstrated what a widespread human habit the drawing of mandalas was. They were in Aztec ruins and Australian Aboriginal traditions; in Hindu artworks, medieval European churches and ancient Chinese texts; in bronze, in stained glass and on parchment; mandalas could be found everywhere once you started looking for them.

Whether they featured an individual human or a cosmic deity at the source, these mandalas, with their big and their small circles and their interior connections, were always a way of touching on some sort of transcendence – a means of connecting with a higher or more whole way of being.

Frequently, the circular design of these mandalas also seemed to express a sense of timelessness, of the eternal truths that lie beyond contingent concerns. Mandalas were involved in the rituals associated with the Australian Aboriginal 'Dreamtime' in which the spirits of past and present meet beyond mortal boundaries. Translated more literally into English, 'Dreamtime' becomes something closer to 'Timelessness'. The circles, wherever and whenever they are found, always seem to be about creating a space that gets beyond the temporal limits and fallibility of normal human life.

Historians and archaeologists think the first mandalas, like the first mazes, were drawn in the sand with fingers or sticks, in the knowledge that they'd soon be wiped from existence by the eternal rhythms of the tide. Tomorrow, you'd have to come back and do it all again, only slightly differently. The basics, the circle and the centre, would remain the same, because the objective was to bring harmony to the whole, with every diverse element united. But the cycle of growth and development – driven by the impossible, yet essential, pursuit of perfect organisational synchronicity and a holistic system – and the new challenges of each day were in perpetual motion.

Whether or not Walt ever heard of a mandala, this definition of one sounds just like his company and its beautifully inked, effortlessly stylish black and red organisational chart, and the timeless classics that were created within its structure, with the red bullseye of 'Direction' the eternal focal point at its centre. The great thing about those first Disney films, and that chart, is that they mean we can all still see first-hand proof of the effectiveness of Walt Disney's machine in all its glory.

Little bee, big buzz

UNTIL THE ADVENT of the software industry, animation was just about the most collaborative creative process imaginable. It involved scores of people working together on the finest details for hundreds of man-hours, to produce every few seconds of on-screen product. In 1935, two years before the release of its debut feature, *Snow White*, the Disney Studio employed 250 people. Yet despite the fact that he wasn't the official director of that film, or of any of the classics that quickly followed (Walt didn't even give himself a production credit), his unmistakable authorial imprint can be seen in every frame of those films. And once Walt's capacity to micromanage the Studio's film-making projects was compromised by his ever-expanding responsibilities within the rapidly growing

Disney empire, his diminished control was equally apparent up there on screen.

Disney's artistic expertise and brilliant management through this golden era were born of his early experiences in the industry – positive and otherwise. Until around 1920, Disney had been an animator, still designing, pencilling and inking complete short films for his burgeoning company.

As the Disney Studio grew and its founder embraced new challenges, he had to find new ways to relate to his employees and new ways for them to work productively with the latest techniques and technologies he was introducing to them. He had to find a way to keep in touch with his films, frame-by-frame, as the workforce, workload and range of specialists under him increased. He had to integrate new technologies and techniques into the work of experienced animation craftspeople without endangering their productivity or prowess. In one interview about his job, Disney likened his role to that of 'a little bee': 'I go from one part of the studio to another and gather pollen and sort of stimulate everybody.'

He certainly generated a buzz, not least among those workers. Effectiveness and efficiency were always on Walt's mind, and therefore were expected of his employees. In an era when there were several talented US studios making great cartoon shorts, the Disney Studio could only thrive if it stayed solvent and competitive at the box office. But this went hand-in-hand with creativity, because the new techniques and tools that he hoped would draw in big audiences also gave animators new challenges to surmount and new vistas for expressing themselves.

talking about things has many virtues, but one of its drawbacks is that it prevents you from getting on and actually doing them. That's why those rare organisations that achieve maximum internal communication and operational clarity with minimal verbiage are so often the very same ones who develop and deliver results most rapidly and efficiently too.

Disney's cartoons were among the first films of any kind to feature sound. Later, the company was key to the introduction of stereo. Thanks to *Snow White*'s majestic songs and Walt's intuitive eye for a parent-friendly new product category, Disney also invented the soundtrack album. In 1932, the company struck a deal with Technicolor for exclusive use of its new three-colour process. Because earlier, two-colour techniques had been so poor, this alliance was great for Disney and Technicolor alike: it gave them a visible superiority with a technology that many rivals had written off as nothing more than a gimmick.

The mandala-like way in which the company was organised meant that potential gimmicks became cinema landmarks. Disney's 'little bee' approach meant that he was able to introduce alien new technologies to in-progress projects and inspire his staff to incorporate them with unmatched artistry. Each person working on every diverse, discrete element of every film had her or his imagination pollinated by Walt's unified vision of the ultimate goal.

Mickey, Donald and ... Oswald?

WALT DISNEY'S DRIVE to productive management was always evident, but he had really learned the importance of finding a way to ensure he had complete oversight back in 1928. The cardinal importance of retaining total control was a painful lesson, but it paved the way for the flawless greatness, and organisational expertise, to come.

In 1927, Universal producer Charles Mintz approached Walt Disney and his studio about creating a series of car-toons featuring a new character called Oswald the Lucky Rabbit. The studio committed itself to the task and worked flat-out to make sure Oswald quickly won an ardent cinema audience. However, it had seemingly slipped Walt's notice that, in the two companies' contract for the show, all rights to the character of Oswald were assigned to Universal. In 1928, Mintz privately approached key animators from the project, asking them to come and continue producing the show at Universal. Only then did Mintz tell Walt Disney of his plan, offering him the choice of either a well-paid job overseeing his poached talent make the Oswald films for Universal or nothing.

Outraged at what he saw as Universal's skullduggery, Disney turned down the job. Instead, in a silver-lining moment worthy of one of his movies, he promptly rechannelled his energies into a new character that would be forever his own. He wasn't a radical departure from what had gone before, but where Oswald had pointy rabbit ears, Walt's replacement had big, round, rodent ones. In 1928, the Disney Studio released *Steamboat Willie*, the screen debut of Mickey Mouse. To the amusement of Disney's associates, Mickey was basically a perpetually cheerful version of Walt – just as Donald Duck, who would arrive six years later, seemed to represent his grizzlier and more manic side. Between them, the characters, soon to be more famous than any human actor, helped ensure that Walt would remain in control from that day forward.

Walt Disney co-directed Mickey's debut in *Steamboat Willie*, but eight years later, when *Snow White* was deep in development, he decided to drop his early plan to direct the Studio's feature-film debut. As one of the first, if not *the* first, animated features ever made, it would be a vast commitment whose failure would sink the studio, however Disney felt his leadership would be put to best use if he took as broad a lens on the film's progress as possible. From that point on, as with the four classics that followed, half the job of each of the men credited with the direction of these peerless movies was simply to work out what Walt wanted, and communicate it to their teams. When they struggled to achieve this, Walt would write concise, insightful memos to individual team members, giving them advice on how to adapt their work in progress.

This template, established in the days of the company's shorts, and refined and extended for its more ambitious features, held good until roughly the time of that organisational chart. After 1943, with Disney deprived of resources in wartime and required to assist with the national propaganda effort, it never quite worked the same way again. After *Bambi*, Disney's next enduring animated feature, *Cinderella*, took eight years to arrive. By then, the Disney Studio's range of documentaries, live-action movies, and Walt's dreams of opening a theme park, were making more and more pressing demands on his time and energy.

Walt Disney died in December 1966. Many of the animated movies that the studio that bore his name had made in his later years had displeased him. He disliked the cost-cutting techniques some animators had used – like the frames from *Bambi* that were recycled in *The Sword in the Stone*, or the Xerox-assisted shorthand animation style that gave the rough edges to the lines of *101 Dalmatians*. Such short-term savings had costs attached – they'd resulted in something Walt never tolerated: a quality-compromising impact on the artistry of the finished film. Less than two decades on from its founder's death, after the Disney family had sold its rights to the studio, the company's latest animated films were even becoming also-rans at the box office, outdone by rival studios welcoming former Disney talent. Walt's once-unbending insistence that technology and efficiency should never compromise quality seemed long forgotten.

The renaissance

THEN, IN 1984, a new regime appointed Michael Eisner as Disney CEO. Eisner promptly set about rejuvenating the company's heritage by overseeing the 'Disney Renaissance'. That's the term now given to the string of winning animated films that followed Eisner's appointment and his establishment of a renewed organisational ethos designed to realign the way the Disney Company was structured to make films and make money. On screen, the fruits of this change – and the first talk of a renaissance – began with 1989's *The Little Mermaid* and continued on with *Beauty and the Beast*, *Aladdin* and *The Lion King*. Eisner went back to Disney's emphasis on market-leading technology, a high-quality bar, timeless stories and great musical scores. But Eisner also followed Walt's appetite for new tools, overseeing the smooth integration of digital techniques into Disney's hand-drawn tradition, inviting contemporary pop stars to make soaring soundtracks that matched the old classics, and making its movies great again – not only at the box office but also in the merchandising arena.

But, as Walt Disney knew, times and technology change, and the best way to stay relevant is to be ahead of everyone else in introducing new technologies to expand your artistry – without ever sacrificing quality or story. By the time Eisner left the company in 2005, Disney's status as the definition of state-of-the art family animation had been usurped by the pioneers at Pixar – film-makers whose success had been financially supported by Disney from the beginning.

Under Eisner, the two companies had been on the verge of breaking up until Walt's nephew, Roy Disney, engineered a boardroom revolt that saw Eisner fired, Bob Iger appointed CEO and Pixar fully integrated into the company. The reason Walt's descendant felt so strongly was, once again, a return to his uncle's first principles. Passing a display of Disney's most beloved characters down the decades, Roy Disney noticed that the new millennium's list was dominated not by characters devised by Disney itself, but by those created at Pixar. Though Disney wasn't doing badly, its bold creative renaissance had petrified into a new formula that felt dated and complacent in ways Walt would never have countenanced.

The future

DISNEY'S FULL ACQUISITION of the computer-animation giant Pixar in 2006 saw John Lasseter become chief creative officer of both Disney and Pixar. One of his first big executive decisions for Disney was to cease development of the inexpensively made straight-to-video sequels Michael Eisner had introduced as a lucrative way of producing revenue for the once-troubled studio. Lasseter understood their financial value but felt that it came at too great a devaluation of the studio's artistic reputation. It was a very Disney thing to do. At the same time, the new CEO Iger focused on acquiring established, top-tier family-entertainment properties to bolster and refresh Disney's unique reputation for quality in that field.

Of course, the definitive and most beloved computer-animated film megahit of modern times was not a Pixar film, even though it took on board many of Pixar's storytelling lessons. With *Frozen*, Disney once again showed the value of balancing classic storytelling and songwriting with new technology for a modern audience. The impact of its visual style and stagey soundtrack has eclipsed even that of the old greats.

Behind every positive and ultimately profitable step in the company's history, Walt's brilliant balancing of creativity and mechanical production still seems detectable. His was a Disney philosophy for the ages.

Pixar:

Art as a Team Sport

EVERY GREAT COMPANY has a 'crunch' story to tell.

It will usually take the form of an epic, 'Can you believe we really did that kind of stuff back then?' character-building tale of absurd deadlines, unavoidable delays and insane overwork from the early days. An almost too incredible account of the mad work binge that might have broken the company but instead helped make it. The test that felt absolutely horrible when it was being taken but made heroes of the people who came through it.

These phases – where everybody is in the office at all hours, working relentlessly to complete a project that's vital to their start-up's future – are almost considered rites of passages for young businesses with aspirations of greatness. And the simple reality is that, if you do claim to strive for excellence, such ordeals are an inevitability.

Almost every enduring company, certainly those in the digital world, has such an epic crunch story, but, just as nobody produces movies quite like Pixar, nobody I know has a crunch story to tell that is quite like theirs.

The year was 1998 and the project was *Toy Story 2*. In keeping with its arrangement with Disney, its key financial ally, Pixar had been developing a straight-to-DVD sequel to the studio's first-ever release, 1995's *Toy Story*, which had been a phenomenal box-office success.

Toy Story 2 was being developed by a discrete team of animators and scriptwriters, working in near-total isolation from the Pixar mother ship. Simultaneously, the company's top creative talent was focused on a separate project, Pixar's second theatrical release and overwhelming priority, the 'insect odyssey' *A Bug's Life*.

One toy, two stories

AT THE TIME this arrangement was entirely sensible: Disney, who had backed Pixar financially since *Toy Story*, had all but invented the market for straight-to-DVD animation. As home video and then DVD took off with consumers, Disney successfully mastered the art of churning out relatively cheap, quick-to-make, albeit inferior, home sequels to its peerless, timeless cinema hits. They sold, though, because they kept the kids quiet, even though they were highly forgettable. Pixar was following that model and the established Disney wisdom by allocating its time and resources accordingly. It was common sense to have its B-team create content that everybody expected to be B-grade.

But in early 1998, when Disney executives first saw some *Toy Story 2* footage during a visit to Pixar, although nobody realised it at the time, they made the call that would shape Pixar's working methods for many years to come.

Thrilled by the early footage from the *Toy Story* sequel, Disney executives decided that, like *A Bug's Life*, this film was too good for straight-to-DVD status. It was worthy of debuting on the big screen.

After this change of direction, both projects continued to proceed independently for several months. The cream of the company was still preoccupied with *A Bug's Life* while the B-team continued working on the now-upgraded *Toy Story 2*. But then, late in 1998, with Disney pushing for confirmation that release dates would be met, the B-team got a visit from Pixar's Braintrust. This was a four-person senior creative panel, including top directors John Lasseter and Andrew Stanton, which had been set up as a crack quality-assurance squad during the evolution of *Toy Story*, the world's first computer-animated feature film. After their visit, the sequence of events that the Braintrust's verdict set in motion reads like a case study designed to prove Friedrich Nietzsche's much-quoted maxim that 'Whatever doesn't kill me makes me stronger'.

Pixar's leadership feared that compromising their creative standards for a quick buck could ruin their plans to build a brand rooted in strict quality controls and unfaltering values. So when Disney insisted in 1998 that *Toy Story 2* would be a cinema-quality release, and had to be ready to open on the big screen for Christmas 1999, Pixar either had to be unpunctual and awkward, in accordance with all the standard creative clichés, or it had to act like a serious, sustainable business and embrace the idea.

The trouble was that, having welcomed Disney's new plan, Pixar's Braintrust only then came to terms with the fact that the work-in-progress on *Toy Story 2*, if it continued as it was, would harm their blossoming reputation, and with it the long-term legacy they craved. So Pixar's management brought all the company's staff together before the Christmas break in 1998 and told them to enjoy it: it was the last meaningful rest they'd have for a year. In 1999, having just finished work on *A Bug's Life*, the company's key talents were moved over to *Toy Story 2* and given a year to turn its script and animation into something truly worthy of Pixar.

The *Toy Story 2* crunch hurt – in all sorts of ways. Several people left the company. Several more got severe, lifelong carpal tunnel conditions and other repetitive strain injuries. Most terrifyingly, one pair of Pixar animators, a married couple, were so exhausted and preoccupied during this peak time that they left their baby locked in their car, windows closed, at the height of summer. Mercifully, they realised in time and their daughter made a swift and full recovery.

As much as the crisis hurt, nobody could realistically blame Disney for it. All Disney had done was decide that *Toy Story 2* looked better than expected and should be upgraded to a full-blown release.

It goes without saying that, with *Toy Story 2*, Pixar created one of the most magical movies, and arguably one of the most beloved sequels, of all time. But the intense period that got them there had caused levels of burnout and heartache they never wanted to repeat. So the first thing the company did after *Toy Story 2* was fix its organisational processes and routines to directly reflect the hard lessons it had learned.

Crunch-proofing the future

PIXAR'S UNYIELDING PRINCIPLES had ensured the company made the right kind of creative impact; the question it now faced was how to maintain those standards without ever returning to such a drastic, desperate phase again. The challenge was to hone an organisational approach that enabled people to do their very best work without risking their health or sanity.

To meet the challenge, Pixar initiated changes and inaugurated new company-wide procedures that were intended to build a better-functioning, less fraught organisation for the future.

For starters, everybody at Pixar was now asked to share what they'd done at work that day with their colleagues. Doing this on a routine daily basis was designed to minimise the chances of last-minute panics, unforeseen problems and long-term misunderstandings. It also tackled the natural human tendency to keep one's work under wraps until it's impressive enough to show off before potentially critical audiences.

The system of daily updates was the most obvious gesture of improved connection and efficiency that followed the *Toy Story* 2 trauma, but there were other crucial steps to eliminate potential bottlenecks and other areas of dysfunction.

For example, during this reorganisational phase, Pixar's management talked independently to the animators, whose job was to bring its films to life, and the production staff, who were responsible for keeping projects on time, on budget and on track. The producers felt like they were resented and regarded as second-class citizens by the animators; the animators admitted, with a degree of embarrassment, that the producers' feelings were pretty much accurate. So these key lines of communication were redrawn and producers and animators alike were encouraged to see each other as parts of the same process, rather than as pests or rivals.

'Anybody should be able to talk to anybody' – that sentiment became one of Pixar's most crucial internal credos following the company's re-formation. Today, if departments don't manage to communicate regularly and respectfully, it's seen as the management's job and urgent priority to establish why, and do whatever it takes to fix it.

Post-mortems can be fun

ANOTHER NEW PILLAR of Pixar's post-*Toy Story* 2 culture was the new and improved post-mortem. Like the idea of meetings to tell your peers what you've achieved that day, post-mortem sessions are something many of us dread.

But like daily progress reports, the trepidation they inspire is a clue to their usefulness. As feeling human beings, we don't want to hear about our failures right after our moment of triumph, but as driven workers, we know that the sooner and more frankly we can diagnose flaws in our last project, the faster and better we can make improvements to our next.

That's why Pixar president Ed Catmull insisted that staff must rigorously adhere to a programme whereby post-mortems swiftly follow the completion of any major production, while the memories of making it were still fresh. In order to prevent staff answering by rote, or playing politics and blame games, he decided that each post-mortem would have a different format, a unique set of questions or some other altered characteristic that stopped those present from glazing over or, in his words, 'gaming the system' instead of giving honest, raw answers.

Those were the new administrative protocols that Pixar's employees now had to abide by. But alongside the imposition of these new rules came a more human, empathetic set of services that staff could opt into for free. Complimentary Pilates, yoga and massage services were introduced after the RSI epidemic on *Toy Story 2*. They cost the company money to provide, of course, but nowhere near as much as they saved in health insurance premiums and reduced medical absenteeism.

But the organisational system that Pixar evolved after *Toy Story 2* had to face up to another dramatic challenge, and arguably its most potentially disruptive yet. Following Disney's $7.4 billion acquisition of Pixar in 2006, the smaller studio's brilliance was acknowledged when Ed Catmull and John Lasseter were given the top creative roles at the new Disney-Pixar. But in return, Disney executives doubled the hit-making studio's release schedule, meaning that the kind of salvage operation The Braintrust did on *Toy Story 2* would never be a practical possibility again.

That might seem a brutal kind of reward for a company that, in two decades, went from being an obscure hardware start-up to the most critically praised and most beloved studio in modern Hollywood. But, as that original *Toy Story 2* crunch team can still testify, Pixar's school of magic-making was never about taking the easy option.

Netflix:

Minimise Rules to Maximise Returns

FEW CONTEMPORARY COMPANIES demonstrate the benefits of organisational audacity quite like Netflix. Today, it's the definition of household name that's an outstanding example of a Limitless approach to business. Yet though it's already an established fixture in so many homes, it's only been going since 1997, when it came out of left field as a plucky, specialist alternative to entrenched rivals who were much bigger and better-resourced.

Those bigger rivals, once household names themselves, dwindled in the twenty-first century, unable to adapt to the new ways people were accessing and consuming entertainment. Netflix, by contrast, evolved and emerged triumphant. It had such a clear and simple objective – to deliver film and television content by the least punitive, most convenient route possible – and had such a finely tuned corporate structure that it was able to adapt and expand masterfully. It first anticipated shifts in the consumption of television, and then engineered shifts in processes and protocols across the whole medium.

In the beginning, commissioning content at Netflix meant ordering thousands of other companies' DVDs. Today, it means funding and developing Emmy-winning drama, documentary, comedy shows and feature films. All along that journey, a core set of philosophies have enabled the brand to expand without sacrificing its identity, and to adapt to a television landscape that was changing faster than anybody had ever anticipated.

Yet it was a journey that might never have happened if it were not for lessons learned from previous mistakes. Reed Hastings, Netflix's co-founder and CEO has explained how his experiences at his first digital business, Pure Software, led him to an obsession with creating the best possible corporate structure for his next venture. 'I had the great fortune of doing a mediocre job at my first company,' he said. 'We got more bureaucratic as we grew.'

Hastings has never been shy about admitting his errors. Having graduated as a prizewinning mathematics student in 1981, he signed up to an officer-training programme with the US Marines before accepting that his compulsive questioning of the way things were done was a bad fit for the armed services. Seeking some other outlet for his urge for adventure, he decided to join the Peace Corps. That led to two years of teaching in Swaziland, before he returned to the US to take a master's degree in computer science at Stanford University.

REED HASTINGS GRADUATED in 1988, then spent a couple of years as a software engineer employed to write bug-checking programmes. Then, in 1991, he and business partner Mark Box founded their own digital services company, Pure Software. The company expanded quickly and, during Hastings's six years in charge, he experienced every kind of complication that comes with early success: a public floatation, drastic fluctuations in share value, multiple arrangements with outside backers and, in 1995, a merger with a competitor. Then, in 1997, the already-merged company was bought out for $750 million by a third software firm, but its value soon plunged. Hastings parted company with Pure Software four months later.

Afforded the opportunity to begin again, Hastings did not want to repeat the experience of starting up a company that he would end up selling off in just a few years – regardless of how wealthy doing so might make him. That's why the money he made from the Pure buyout went straight back into an ambitious new idea.

Hastings didn't want to rush into the wrong future, or repeat the same mistakes he'd made before. As he later said, he had only really been a glorified 'engineer' for most of his time at Pure – a technocrat running a company according to abstract, but comfortingly clear-cut, systems and strategies. He wanted his next business to engage with the nuances of human behaviour and motivation that make a company tick. He also wanted to build something that was founded on a future-proof proposition, with an organisational structure so well designed that it could scale up without getting slowed, or watered down and attract investment without compromising its identity. He wanted to build a Limitless business, and so began to learn how to be a CEO worthy of the title.

Pushing the envelope

THE BUSINESS HASTINGS built was, of course, Netflix. Founded in 1997, in partnership with fellow Pure Software alumnus Mark Randolph, the new firm, based in Los Gatos, California, was to be a more coherent and effective breed of organisation. This drive for joined-up thinking started with the name; though it was a DVD-rental business, Hastings didn't want to call the company something that would tie it to any one particular technological format. Instead, he combined the name for the key entertainment delivery technology of the new century with an old word for cinema-going that dated from the early, flickery days of celluloid. 'Netflix' cleverly ensured the company would be primed for change if and when niche experiments like video downloads and online streaming grew in importance and feasibility.

In its first year, the name Netflix seemed about the most unusual thing about the young company. Its only initial innovation was that it allowed these familiar transactions to take place from the comfort of the customer's PC; it still charged late fees and rental charges on the established high-street model. However, just a few months in, the nascent company experimented with a trial subscription programme. Instead of traditional return dates and accompanying fines, the new mail-order service asked subscribers to request movies, await their arrival, then return them as and when they chose by prepaid surface mail.

The new system meant people might wait a while for certain titles to come through to them, but early adopters generally accepted that as an understandable side effect of the new fine-free flexibility they all enjoyed. There was always something to watch, and there was never anything extra to pay. The Netflix customer base exploded and started doubling every month. It was a pioneering on-demand service: half-analogue and half-digital, like the 'Netflix' name, and supposedly inspired by a $40 fee Hastings himself had once been hit with for the late return of a single DVD rental.

That all sounds terribly old-fashioned now, of course – something that is in large part a tribute to how rapidly Netflix has transformed the industry. As its new service took off, Netflix represented a revolution in customer-focused policies and service, in a sector that had historically shown minimal interest in the convenience of its customers. The new fixed-fee system – and the freedom from nasty, unexpected late charges that came with it – made it clear that Netflix was a company intent on breaking with the old, punitive ways. Here was a brand boldly refusing to perpetuate the system of rental as ransom. That gave people a reason to root for its success rather than resent it, and in its first year almost a quarter of a million Americans signed up for the novel online subscription service. From that point forward, the number of Netflix subscribers surged and its profile soared.

That's why, by the early 2000s, far bigger and more established companies were trying to muscle in on the upstart's act. First up was Wal-Mart, which announced its mail-order rental service in 2002, swiftly resulting in a $2.50 drop in the Netflix share price and two years of competition in the sector. But in 2005, the supermarket giant admitted defeat, refocused on retailing DVDs rather than renting them out, and resumed civilised relations by easing into a mutually beneficial promotional arrangement with Netflix.

The other entrenched brand that Hastings and his new, 20-person company had to stare down was Blockbuster – a household name with over 9,000 outlets, 60,000 staff, 6,000 automated DVD vending machines, a market valuation worth billions and literally tens of millions of customers in the US. It was a competitor Hastings took seriously – after all, market analysts at the time argued that there would only be one winner in the DVD-by-mail wars. Most of these experts believe well-resourced Goliaths like Amazon or Blockbuster would be almost certain to secure that title.

If you can't join them, beat them

IN FACT, JUST a few months after Netflix launched its game-changing subscription model, Reed Hastings had sought to join Blockbuster instead of competing against the giant rival. Hastings had never underestimated the battle that such a massive and well-known incumbent would give Netflix. That's why, once the subscription model had proved its worth, his first move was to offer to partner Netflix with Blockbuster. In the summer of 2000, Hastings flew to Blockbuster's Dallas headquarters to meet CEO John Antioco and make him a business proposition: if Blockbuster would invest $50 million in Netflix and create in-store displays for its services, Netflix would run – would *become* – Blockbuster's online rental network.

The video giant heard Hastings out, but didn't seriously entertain the proposition. Instead Blockbuster later launched a DVD-by-mail service of its own.

However, never resting on its laurels, Netflix was proven to be one step ahead of its rivals with its next innovation. At the beginning of 2007 it launched an Internet streaming service, which was well established by the time Blockbuster launched its own rivalling service. By the end of 2007 the Blockbuster service had 3 million subscribers, meanwhile Netflix continued to expand its customer base exponentially.

By the end of the 2000s, the strategic disputes that had plagued Blockbuster left it divided and facing plunging revenues. Because so much of its costs were tied up in bricks and mortar, the company's management focused on trying to keep the physical business afloat, despite the glaring evidence that consumers were increasingly shunning DVDs by mail and heading online for their rented entertainment.

In September 2010, Blockbuster LLC filed for Chapter 11 bankruptcy protection. The following year, Blockbuster was auctioned for a mere $320 million. However, the change of management couldn't turn back the tide; the new owners ended up closing more stores than they'd first anticipated, and by November 2013 they announced that they were closing Blockbuster's DVD-by-mail service as well as the remaining stores, while maintaining an on-demand service.

Like so many once-great entertainment empires that have been undone by digital, Blockbuster was encumbered by its sheer size, overheads on the high street, and the legacy of its once-successful business model being so inextricably invested in particular hardware formats. But the success of Netflix was not simply a matter of good timing. Netflix outlived and outflanked rivals and out-thought industry analysts because it is a brilliantly structured company. The team was organised and incentivised to make smart, swift, independent decisions that accelerated the company's progress towards its clear long-term aims.

'FREEDOM & RESPONSIBILITY' is the name Netflix gives to the company's unique internal culture and code of conduct. Think the name sounds a little utopian? Suspiciously sugar-coated? As usual, Reed Hastings, the mastermind who wrote it, has already anticipated that. The lean staff hand-book itself confronts that very concern on the first page, by pointing out the gulf between Enron's noble stated values and its sticky, nefarious end. From there, Hasting's docu-ment sets out exactly how a company structure can create a culture where what's said is the same as what's done:

> 'Real company values are the behaviours and skills that we particularly value in fellow employees.'

Which pretty much takes us back to the *shokunin* spirit, and, before that, Aristotle's insistence that

> 'We are what we repeatedly do. Excellence, then, is not an act, but a habit'.

The Netflix staff guidelines are less about dictating what to do, and more about explaining *why* fewer instructions enable individuals to take on more meaningful responsibility.

Hastings' innovative guidelines are rooted in his belief that creative people can easily be forced out by excessive oversight and responsibility. He further believes that the best people are twice as productive as average at procedural work, and ten times more productive than average at creative work. So the Netflix organisational objective has always been to engineer the kind of culture in which staff can be given the freedom to be creative, while simultaneously taking on the responsibility to keep the company, its budgets and practical necessities on track.

Famously, there are no rules about employee-paid holiday entitlements. As the handbook says, Netflix doesn't count hours worked – because it doesn't make sense to do so in an era when people answer emails on mobile devices on their weekends, evenings, commutes and, yes, even on holiday. By extension, it makes no sense to have strict, school-style rules on time off. So, since 2004, Netflix hasn't had any at all – holiday rules that is. If an employee wants to take a couple of days or a couple of weeks off they are free to do so – no questions asked and no records kept. They are, of course, still held accountable for their goals being met on time. It's not a free-for-all but, instead, a highly leveraged, trust-based employee–employer relationship.

While wages at Netflix are above the industry average, they are also tied to the performance of the company and the wider market. Employees are encouraged to ask around the industry to ensure they aren't being undervalued. They're also told the opposite of what every good schoolchild is told: that lots of work is 'not directly relevant' to getting ahead. The emphasis is not on doing the 'right thing' so much as doing whatever yields the right result for the company.

Such selected HR highlights do sometimes make Netflix sound like a fantasy version of office life. But, in their entirety, Hastings's guidelines make it abundantly clear why such unlikely ideas underpin the foundations of a relentlessly innovative, $50 billion-dollar company. Pay is high so that people are attracted and motivated and market-based, so it's fair for all. Severance pay is above average so that managers don't feel bad about letting merely 'adequate' performers go, and an employee has to be rated a 'superstar' in their current role to be considered for promotion. Symbolic 'hard work', like staying at your desk until all hours, isn't rewarded because results and 'productiveness under deadline' are the only metrics of employee value that count for the business.

If you love somebody, set them free

THE 'FREEDOM & Responsibility' guide demands creative disputes and straight talk in the name of frank decision-making. Its few explicit prohibitions include using the free-speaking environment to play politics, or indulging 'brilliant jerks' whose talent is not worth their egotism and selfishness. Both pose a danger to a minimalist administrative system rooted in frankness and mutual respect.

Because, as Hastings writes, 'there *is* a system.' The fact that the Netflix system is designed on a presumption of trust and transparency by no means makes it a soft, woolly one. Hasting's Freedom & Responsibility policy constitutes a hard operational argument about management theory and the ideal balance of regulation and innovation.

Within the pages of his guidelines, Hastings sketches the two conventional twentieth-century models of corporate organisation at scale. One kind of company is tightly regimented, big on oversight and short on innovation, where every worker and department is drilled to work and interact within a minutely prescribed set of rules, checks and balances to prevent disaster. The other kind of company is the freer-form type made up of inward-looking 'independent silos', each pursuing localised goals. That can mean more freedom, and freedom to make mistakes, but can also lead to wasted resources and conflicting internal goals.

Reed Hastings decided he wanted to have it both ways. He wasn't willing to settle for the traditional alternatives of either a lazy, loose system or a hyper-controlled machine. Netflix is organised to be a 'loosely aligned, tightly coupled' system in which people are free to act on their initiative, but get to do so within a framework that ensures their objectives coincide with those of the company. In other words, when big changes happen, everybody should be in a position to pull together to make the most of them.

Practically speaking, that means regular scheduled inter-group meetings and regular scheduled site updates, so nothing ever needs to be prepared or repaired in a panic. Managers are given freedom to spend their budget as they see fit and are expected to assume the responsibility to ensure they don't exceed it. Overspend in one department in one quarter necessitates meetings for reallocation of resources to rebalance in the next – in other words, if you're financially undisciplined, your failure leads to more meetings, and there will be no way of ignoring that it's all your fault. Just as at Pixar, robust post-mortems are seen as essential to progress.

Freedom naturally means occasional mistakes, but, as the handbook pointedly states, 'We're in a creative-inventive-market, not a safety-critical market like medicine or nuclear power.' Hastings believes that the kind of high-performance people Netflix wants as employees are precisely the kind of people who leave a company once it becomes over-regulated and slow.

If a company wants to keep such people, it has to trust them and give them opportunities to excel and innovate. Hastings argues that such high-performers make very few mistakes if they're treated properly and committed to the cause. He also points out that, in a creative environment, it isn't necessarily cheaper to prevent an accident than it is to quickly remedy it. Missing out on an opportunity altogether can be far worse for a creative business than temporarily messing up an experimental new idea.

When Reed Hastings started Netflix, he wanted to build a better kind of business. When streaming became a viable option, he wanted to be the leader in the field. And when he was asked in 2007 what he'd like to do once he'd fought off his giant rivals, Hastings said that he would love to become a beloved brand like HBO. Within six years, Netflix had done just that, becoming a powerhouse producer of acclaimed television programming, and, in the Winter of 2013, eclipsing HBO's total US subscriber numbers for the first time in its history.

The joy of data

IN 2013, AT the Edinburgh International Television Festival's MacTaggart lecture, the Oscar-winning actor Kevin Spacey talked about the funding of his Emmy-winning miniseries *House of Cards*, the first of a series of superior new drama and comedy serials that Netflix launched that year:

> Netflix was the only network that said, 'We believe in you. We've run our data and it tells us that the audience would watch this series. We don't need you to do a pilot. How many episodes do you want to do?'

Spacey was talking about the political drama series in which he starred, but, more broadly, he was also talking about the importance of Netflix as a model for sustaining high-quality television as a viable business. With a reasonable, fair-charging model and convenient delivery, Spacey argued, the television industry could avoid the fate that befell the recorded music business when record sales trailed off while gigs and merchandise became the main source of income.

Some critics saw Spacey's talk as a little ahead of itself. Others sniped when Netflix declined to release conventional viewing figures for the first series of *House of Cards*. But by the time the second series was released in early 2014, the update of an old BBC drama had become one of the most talked-about shows in the English-speaking world. When the established TV networks announced 2014's line-up of pilots for potential new shows, *Variety* did a cover story on the drastic change in approach that season. The networks' spend on pilots was down 15 per cent year-on-year, but, on the plus side, more new shows were being commissioned direct for entire series. Once again, Netflix had led the way, and made the greatest gains by moving first. What was new was how directly its innovations were taken up by its long-established competition.

Netflix never had to rely on those brutal, wasteful old ways like pilots, because it has always put its trust in its data. It predicts what its customers will want to do next, rather than abiding by outmoded industry protocols. Typically, Hastings's new appetite for programme-making came good at just the right time because the costs of the back-catalogue movies that were once the bread and butter of Netflix continue to rise with diminishing returns as rivals splash out to compete.

As well as crunching the numbers on what its customers watch and will watch, Netflix keeps track of illegal download charts to get a full picture of what people are interested in. But its creative strategies are by no means dictated by data; the company also trusts in new writing and directorial talent in ways traditional TV networks can no longer afford to. Those networks, like the cable channels and Hollywood studios, will all sit up when the lean Netflix machine reveals its next ahead-of-the-curve innovation. Ratings or no ratings, rules or no rules, in the battle for eyeballs, it's good to know everybody's watching you.

Nike:

The Organisation as Athlete

'IF YOU HAVE a body, you are an athlete.' As a storied and deeply respected sports coach, Bill Bowerman made that statement from a position of some experience. As co-founder of Nike, he helped make it the foundation of a new kind of business – one that is still breaking rules and making records half a century later.

Despite its vintage, that statement, 'If you have a body, you are an athlete', has lost none of its power to make you sit up. And that is the whole point: it's a call for everybody to realise their potential; a reminder that every moment of every day is an opportunity for improvement and advancement. It's an injunction to strive and see what you're capable of, instead of cautiously or cockily resting on your laurels.

As such, it's a belief that not only inspires Nike's ever-growing customer base, but also enables those within the company to keep innovating and experimenting as it expands. It's the essence of Nike's organisational ethos, the model through which its leaders have kept the company healthy, innovative and high-achieving.

Just as *corporare*, the Latin root of the word 'corporation', means 'combine in one body', so, too, the root of our
word 'organisation' stems from the metaphor of the human
anatomy. A good business is not just a schematic puzzle
but a living, evolving thing.

*the best coaches, like the greatest athletes, understand the
strange truth that achieving consistent excellence is about
maintaining a perpetual outlook of apprenticeship.*

The idea of the athlete unites the numerous free-flow-
ing and unconventional elements of Nike's internal culture
around a single sensibility. It's the enduring reference point
that enables Nike to encourage experimentation without
endangering its momentum or muddying its sense of
direction.

One key reason the athlete is such a useful touchstone
for an organisation is that the ultimate goals of any sport,
at any level, are absolutely clear at all times: outscore your
opponent, beat your personal best, take your team towards
victory by making sure it scores more goals than your
rivals.

Such unambiguous objectives aren't usually so easy to
find in the average business. And because the goals of athletes are so pure, simple and straightforward, it's always in

their interest to be open-minded about anything that can provide an advantage, however unlikely or unproven. Unlike many process- and protocol-bound employees, athletes are free to experiment with and explore any novel approach that might conceivably bring them closer to those goals. As such, they set an organisational marker for businesses that want to stay imaginative, competitive, creative and relevant.

At Nike, there's a second reason the idea of the athlete has been such a potent organisational influence. From the company's earliest origins, the 'athlete' ideal has always had its critical counterpart in the concept of the 'coach': the person who exists to make the talented athlete into a great one, to turn prospects into fulfilment, and to drill into their charges the idea that success is a reason to try even harder next time. Having a body may make you an athlete, but it doesn't get you a coach. Coaching is the crucial difference not only between amateur athletes and elite athletes, but also that between elite performers in sports and their elite counterparts in other professions, such as medicine or classical music, where star performers are usually largely left to practice and learn on their own once they've completed their initial education.

The coach is the living expression of the idea that we all always remain students, or should do; that none of us ever has 'nothing left to learn'. Embracing the concept of coaching means having the humility to accept that we are all works in progress, and never quite will be finished articles.

If you abandon the idea that you already know it all, you can begin to celebrate that learning and growing on the job is what makes life and entrepreneurship worthwhile; it's how you make every day feel different, instead of lapsing into lazy routine. The best coaches, like the greatest athletes, understand the strange truth that achieving consistent excellence is about maintaining a perpetual outlook of apprenticeship.

Competitive advantage

PHIL KNIGHT WAS a committed and capable college-level runner, one whose educational career and passion for sport brought him into the orbit of exceptional athletes and coaches. Knight was an accomplished University of Oregon track runner who got interested in buying and selling shoes while studying for his MBA at Stanford. There, in 1962, he wrote an economically astute paper about the high cost of imported running shoes and the related opportunity for a new entrant in the market.

As if determined to prove his academic thesis in the real world of commerce, Knight soon used his knowledge and love of both sport and business to create his own athletic footwear company with his college track coach, Bill Bowerman.

Established in January 1964 as Blue Ribbon Sports, the company started out by importing high-quality, lower-cost running shoes from Japan. Within a few years, the firm had moved into creating and producing its own designs under the new name of Nike (new to sporting goods but, of course, not to Greek mythology). The string of radical design and organisational innovations that followed Knight and Bowerman's start-up set the organisation on the road to the 'category of one' status it enjoys today.

From the outset, Knight wanted to create a business where passion and intensity ran as deeply in managers and staff as it did in star athletes. He wanted to inspire his employees to greater things the same way his favourite coach had inspired him. That's why he had asked his college track coach to co-found the business with him, and why Bowerman's wisdom has always been such a crucial contributor to the Nike sensibility.

Bowerman's track record as a coach was remarkable; he provided hands-on instruction to no less than 33 US Olympians in his time. His feats as an innovator were no less impressive. Relentless in search of techniques and tools that would help his runners to make strides, he once said that the ideal running shoe 'would provide enough support for a runner during a race, but would fall apart once that runner crossed the finish line'. With the focus on helping his athletes achieve their full potential, Bowerman invented the cushioned wedge heel in 1967. Five years later, he created a new, lighter and grippier kind of rubber sneaker sole with a tool taken from his home kitchen.

Fuelled by innovation and a changing America, at a time in which the country was moving increasingly to sports participation and overall fitness, Nike laid the foundations of a new, dynamic growth industry that supplanted a separate series of sectors – shoes, clothing and sporting goods – in which progress had historically been slow.

Leading the field

PHIL KNIGHT WAS never a rule-crazed, protocol-bound kind of leader. Long before the trend of transparency, in the early days he encouraged staff meetings that were as open, frank, boisterous and robust as any professional-level competitive team sport. This provided the freedom for them to challenge and provoke the status quo, to have heated discussions, to suggest the unthinkable at every opportunity.

there's no substitute for ongoing coaching, and more of us should learn from the handful of elite performance fields where everybody already realises and accommodates that truth.

Years after the company had become a multimillion-dollar business, staff could recount how Knight's eyes would glaze over the moment someone's prized slide presentation was booted up for his edification. Another famous aversion of Knight's was to the use of lots of words when one, or none, would suffice – a tendency so pronounced that, over time, staff who went to see him with new ideas learned to take his silence as a green light for getting on with things, rather than a condemnation. Though it should be noted that this didn't mean the anxieties of staff *completely* ended when they felt they had Knight's tacit approval. He did prefer them to stay on their toes; after all, this is the man who famously insisted, 'I reserve the right to change my mind tomorrow.'

All-time record

THE IDEA OF the athlete succinctly expressed a company-wide love of the exhilaration, competition, collaboration and manifold satisfactions of participating in sport. Just as Knight was a runner, so today's CEO and President, Mark Parker, who joined Nike in 1979, ran competitively. By no means everyone at the company can boast of such sporting achievements, but they are all utterly in tune with the principles behind them.

Knight reinforced this association between his corporate goals and athletic aspirations by channelling his love of sports into a celebration of great athletic achievers. As Nike's footwear design and marketing teams helped create the era of the modern superstar athlete, Knight made the relationship reciprocal by bringing these luminaries to the company's headquarters and outposts and getting them to address, mingle, inspire and collaborate with the people who worked there.

At Nike, an education never really ever ends. Its people work in buildings named after the world-beating athletes the brand has partnered with down the years: Michael Jordan, Mia Hamm, John McEnroe, and many more legends besides. Employees at the Nike campus are constantly reminded where the company came from by the defining moments of its history, as evoked by the memorabilia dotted around its facilities. Perhaps the most striking of all these relics and trophies is still the humble waffle iron, plundered from its prior role in the Bowermans' kitchen, with which Bill Bowerman invented that running sole.

Game changer

BUT THE IDEA of the athlete isn't just about historical achievements or a romantic respect for the people who made today's Nike possible. The athlete's ethos is also a living, breathing and entirely practical philosophy. Over the past 40 years, a substantial body of academic research has singled out key shared characteristics that set great athletes apart from the rest of us. Five characteristics, in particular, have been repeatedly identified:

1. High motivation and commitment
2. A self-confident, optimistic outlook on the world
3. A positive-minded pursuit of perfection
4. A strong ability to focus and refocus
5. A greater ability to manage adversity and stress.

In other words, athletes pursue their goals like everybody's dream company or employee. But even though those characteristics of positivity, discipline, a competitive spirit and motivation predispose a person to athletic success, they in no sense guarantee it will happen. The entire nature of elite sporting achievement is that there can never be a magic formula for attaining it, however much we want to believe there might be.

And we do seem to want to believe. We look for magic formulas for sporting success, even though history shows us this is folly. As soon as a radical idea becomes a new training orthodoxy, as soon as one team or one athlete's successful experiment hardens into an inflexible ideology for others, it becomes vulnerable to becoming undone. The 'Moneyball' philosophy saw the Oakland A's transform their baseball fortunes by using performance data to pick playing personnel, in a story that became a 2003 book and then a 2011 movie. But the team's success meant rival teams realised what they were missing and established their own evidence-based selection systems, which in turn negated the Oakland A's once game-changing point of difference.

There was considered a 'right' way to sprint – with your knees high and your strides wide, until 1996 when Michael Johnson became the only man to win the 200-metre and 400-metre races at a single Olympics, with a running style that broke all the rules – and which early coaches had tried to 'correct'. There was also a *right* way to serve in tennis

– underarm – until the second Wimbledon tournament, in 1878, when one A.T. Myers decided to serve overarm, quickly precipitating a change not only in the approach of other players, but also in the standard height of the net.

The endurance race

THAT'S WHY COACHES such as Bill Bowerman always worked with the empirical proofs of a day on the track, rather than putting their faith in an eternal law. There is no rule that lasts for the ages, because sports, science and human bodies are always evolving. There is no magic number of hours after which you have 'mastered' an athletic discipline. Once you believe in a rule absolutely, you're prone to stop observing. That's why the restless inquisitiveness of the coach, trying in every way to find new ways to enhance the athlete's achievement and advantage, remains such a valuable reference point.

In one of his most influential essays, doctor, public health researcher and bestselling author Atul Gawande asked why it was only athletes and singers who continued to work with coaches after they succeeded in their fields. After a chance encounter with a tennis coach had instantly improved a serve that Gawande had long regarded as the strongest part of his game, he realised that, even in his late forties, there was no reason why his ability at tennis couldn't improve rather than decline. This made him ask why surgeons and other elite professionals were considered the complete article after their formal training, and left to maintain their own abilities thereafter. Gawande conducted an experiment where he invited a fellow surgeon to watch a recording of him performing a thyroidectomy and make observations about his work afterwards. This was an operation he'd done over a thousand times – yet he said that his colleague's feedback 'gave me more to consider and work on than I'd had in the past five years.' Gawande concluded that there's no substitute for ongoing coaching, and more of us should learn from the handful of elite performance fields where everybody already realises and accommodates that truth.

there is no more beautiful trophy than longevity.

The best coaches are such prized alchemists at converting potential into attainment. Like great managers, they try to nurture talent by guiding those who possess it to achieve as much as they possibly can; they adapt to their charges, and their limits and possibilities of the human body, rather than trying to shoehorn individuals into a pre-existing system regardless. This guiding role is more about instilling simple, *shokunin*-style disciplines and thought processes as it is about imposing grand theories or rigidly obeying statistics.

Algorithms and magic numbers for achievement come and go, but five decades on from the founding of Nike, the athlete–coach connection is at the core of its ever-expanding interests and willingness to experiment, rather than sticking with proven successes.

Harder, better, faster, stronger

SOME OF THE greatest athletes to be graced by the Nike swoosh owe their legends to the way they adapted their games as they matured and their natural strength and speed had to be supplemented by new approaches to tactics and training. Despite having won World and European Cups with France by the age of 22, and playing in a forward position where injury and early retirement are more common, Thierry Henry played on until he was 37, adapting his game to the changing demands of his body and avidly embracing the new footballing cultures of the places he moved to. Asked at the time of his retirement if longevity was the hardest thing to achieve in football, he agreed. But he added:

> it's also the ultimate accolade – especially when you're a striker, with all the young guys coming through. It's not just a question of staying power, it is also an obligation to perform. There is no more beautiful trophy than longevity. To stay at the same level, when people are expecting so much at each game ... Ronaldo, Messi ... Are people really aware of what they do, of their consistency of performance? Do they realise how tough it is to be always at the top?

AT TODAY'S NIKE the combined DNA of athlete, coach and entrepreneur ensures that the pace of innovation is healthier and stronger than ever. Its responsiveness and adaptability are the reason that it's gained such a foothold. A year short of its half century, in 2013, the business was dubbed the world's 'Most Innovative' by Fast Company. In 2016 Nike's CEO Mark Parker was named Businessperson of the Year by *Fortune* magazine. There's also been a startling upswing in the rate at which Nike has expanded its already-unrivalled roster of patents, with year-over-year increases of more than 60 per cent.

Those patents covered everything from new kinds of digital sensor systems for teams and individuals to shoes that automatically lace up to heat-sensitive golf balls. Since 1976, Nike has racked up more than four times the number of patents of its rivals. Phil Knight's company has changed and grown in almost every imaginable respect since Nike first set out to introduce new perspectives to the circumscribed field of running shoes, but its drive to pursue the next frontier – rather than settling for the finish line – has not.

It is in the nature of people to be fearful of change and to resist the different or the new. Yet it is variation and modification in an athlete's training regime that opens up the most exciting new prospects and yields the most consistent gains in sporting performance. It is in the nature of championship athletes that they are rarely satisfied – hence

Nike executives' championing of the positive contribution that can be made by a spirit of 'constant dissatisfaction'.

'When we commit to the athlete's potential,' Phil Knight always liked to tell the teams that made Nike run, 'we realise our own'.

Samsung:

Constant Striving

ONE STORY ABOUT Samsung so perfectly encapsulates the brand's enduring strengths that, even though it is actually true, it instantly acquired the staying power of myth after it was first told in a Korean financial newspaper in 2002.

Once upon a time, a group of Samsung workers were scheduled to move a consignment of delicate machinery for constructing semiconductors from one of the company's facilities to another. But on their commutes into work early on the designated day, some of the group noticed that the road that connected the two plants had been damaged and could well pose a threat to the safe transit of the fragile equipment.

Rather than wait for the state authorities to respond to the problem, the workers went out to the site of the damage, equipped with supplies gathered at their Samsung plant, and resurfaced the road themselves with new tarmac. With the many Samsung domestic electric fans they'd also brought along, they then blasted the new stretch of road surface with air to accelerate the drying process. Within a few hours, the unforeseen problem was remedied, and the

Samsung workers were able to complete the day's crucial delivery of fragile equipment right on schedule.

That story crystallises the absolute focus on delivery and execution, on personal humility and collective sensibility, which has shaped Samsung (which means 'three stars') since its foundation in 1938. There's never been a 'That's not my job' syndrome there. As Intel's former Executive Vice President Sean M. Maloney put it more recently:

> When Samsung wants to get something done, the decision comes down from the top and everybody moves at lightning-quick speed to just do it.

For the bulk of Samsung's eight decades of existence, this shared drive and can-do mentality was a necessity for corporate survival. For most of that time, Samsung was as a supplier of electronic components and a producer of discount electrical goods. This meant that, throughout its history, the company had to constantly forage for meagre new margins and to do its best to prevent the generic commodities it produced from being undercut or outpaced by its numerous, equally hungry and efficiency-driven competitors.

Applied to and adapted for the twenty-first century, this founding ethos of 'aggressive investment and speed' became the 'sashimi theory' expounded by former Samsung CEO Jong-Yong Yun. In essence it says that, in the digital age, electronic consumer goods lose value at the same rapid pace as raw fish. It's a vivid – some might even say pungent – metaphor. After all, any cut of fish that graces Jiro Ono's sushi plate at this moment will only be fit for his waste bin in an hour, let alone tomorrow.

The tarmac highways have been eclipsed by the information highways, but the do-what-it-takes approach through which Samsung survived the countless challenges of its first decades is the same one that transformed the company's fortunes and its image in the digital era.

Survival – the great motivator

LIKE REED HASTINGS, Samsung's founder Lee Byung-chull learned first-hand about organisational failings from his first start-up. He then applied the hard-learned lessons at his next company, the one that made him a legend. At 26, Byung-chull set up a rice-milling business in his native province of Kyungnam with money he had inherited from his late father, a wealthy land-owner. When that failed, he relocated to Daegu, in the south-east of the country with the aim of building a business that lasted. Precisely what the nature of the business would be was a secondary concern; he just needed to make sure the business was doing something – anything – that brought in income.

So that second company, Samsung, started out as an export and logistics business moving goods for brands. Seeing his products and understanding his supply chains enabled Byung-chull to extend Samsung's portfolio of businesses into all sorts of new areas and undercut rivals. In the early days, he experimented with a wide variety of sidelines, constantly refining or replacing them if they didn't prove viable. If a new opportunity for making a profit arose, Lee was determined that Samsung must be poised and prepared to be the first to exploit it. As he built up a small but growing workforce, that was the defining quality he needed in his people: instant adaptability to a new directive or opportunity.

Humane resources

WAY BEFORE IT was fashionable (or even advisable) to say such things, Lee insisted that his people were Samsung's most important project. The big idea through which he conveyed Samsung's grand strategy to those employees was the concept of *muhantamgu*, which translates as 'constant striving' or 'infinite quest'. *Muhantamgu* is now the motto of Samsung's research and development group.

This was a crucial and instantly understood message for his employees. The Korea in which Lee and his first generation of staff had come of age was a rural country undergoing a rapid, state-driven process of industrialisation. However, that process was severely handicapped by the country's dependence on more powerful neighbours like Japan and China. Access to international resources and expertise was therefore limited and unreliable. If you wanted to get anything done, then the ability to capitalise on what little *was* available was a crucial skill – doing it with harmony and humility was an art form.

Muhantamgu was very different to the similarly spiritual Japanese concept of the *shokunin*, because in practice it didn't entail a sense of pride in the end product as a perfected object. That kind of rarefied crafting ethos was a luxury that Korean businesses didn't have at the time. Samsung's striving was not about the resolved satisfactions of great design, but more about the immense difficulty of merely surviving against better-positioned, better-equipped and deep-pocketed foreign rivals. In essence, it was about making something from next to nothing.

So the company went from brokering industrial components to manufacturing its own, and finding efficiencies in production and supply chains in order to undercut its rivals in the sector. Then, in 1969, Samsung Electronics was founded. The plan was to take advantage of the era's boom in consumer gadgets – a period during which companies such as Sony had flourished – but Samsung's engineers had no access to the know-how or equipment required to actually make anything. Samsung valiantly dispatched teams to visit leading Japanese companies to try to solve the supply problem and forge partnerships with those in the know. However, nobody ever seemed to want to help, and it was not until 1974 that the Japanese brand Panasonic (then known as Matsushita Electric Industrial Co.), finally agreed to supply them with the parts that enabled the production of the first Samsung TV set.

In 1982, Lee Byung-chull made his last and perhaps most audacious and legendary management decision of all: he decided that the company should commit to expanding its production of digital chip sets, despite the training and building that would be required. Lee sensed that digital memory would play a major part in the future, and it was Samsung's ahead-of-the-curve emphasis on making DRAM chips, which packed in more memory than the market-leading chips of the time, that finally made them an admired industry leader.

However, like rice or grain, digital memory was still a commodity. It was a product for which the price was dictated by market forces, not brand positioning or design values. In this respect, it was no different to the kind of second-tier consumer goods for which Samsung Electronics would become increasingly known in the 1980s and 1990s.

The last aspires to be first

BECAUSE THE COMPANY'S leaders were more concerned with survival than status, they were open to exploring every angle and were relentlessly focused on achieving more effective outcomes. The company collectively strived so tirelessly that it laid the foundations for its metamorphosis from supplier to creator, copycat to a trendsetter, sniffed-at second-tier brand to inspirational segment leader.

Digital was the shift Samsung succeeded at because the company understood the unique opportunity that the transition from analogue to digital presented. The digitisation of consumer electronics during the 1990s and early 2000s completely rewrote the rules of research, engineering, design and branding for mass-market technology companies. The long-standing criteria according to which consumers perceived and purchased electronic goods were suddenly changed. Anticipating this change, Samsung grabbed its opportunity to finally compete with leading brands on a level playing field, thereby morphing into a company whose products could command premiums, instead of competing on price alone. This was Samsung's chance to become a leader, instead of a follower.

In the analogue age, customer loyalty had come naturally to discerning purchasers of electronic goods. If you were a home-entertainment buff, or even a repair man, you'd champion Sony's patented Trinitron technology because their television sets were built to last and their unique components meant a sharper, better-coloured picture every time. The difference was self-evident in the detail of performance, as well as in other important areas, such as style and build quality.

the absolute focus on delivery and execution, on personal humility and collective sensibility.

Back then, the huge gulf between a handful of revered global leaders and the hundreds of low-profile Asian and European brands offering discount versions of the front-runners' innovations seemed insurmountable.

Digital changed all that. Firstly, because it naturally tended to generate industry-wide quality standards, like shared coding languages and screen technology, as well as universal software formats such as JPEG and MP3. Secondly, because it put the power in the one place where Samsung's adaptability and drive had already established it as a market leader: the chip. A new dawn of digital cameras, televisions, tablets and even toasters all owed their key functions to a single chip set, and Samsung's striving made it singularly prepared for the shift.

Digital – *the great equaliser*

THAT SINGLE CHIP structure meant that different manufacturers, of vastly differing historical reputations, quickly found themselves making competing devices that were all powered by the same technology and therefore all delivering comparable results. A nimble, rigorous entrant into a market could learn and acquire the right components with such ease that they could make a disruptive, competitive impact on the establishment leaders – and do it quickly.

Samsung realised this opportunity and readied itself to take advantage. Supply chains were refined until they were responsive and efficient. Sales representatives invested vast quantities of time and great distances travelling to forge exceptional distribution relationships, so that Samsung's products could elevate themselves from discount stores to the same prestige placements enjoyed by rivals like Sony, Pioneer and Panasonic.

Although nobody paid the company a great deal of attention, the legwork being undertaken day in, day out by Samsung's loyal legions, slowly, surely made a difference. In 2002, a Sony executive reportedly commented that, 'We still believe that Samsung is basically a component company.' If the executive in question had checked the Korean 'component' company's market valuation later that year, he would have observed that it had eclipsed that of his own.

Because it had no illustrious product-development history to hark back to, Samsung quickly outpaced established electronics firms – not least Sony – in leading the transition from analogue TV sets to flat LCD and plasma panels. While Sony and others were left with unsold stocks of CRTs and outdated facilities, Samsung was overwhelmed with demand for the flat-screen technologies to which it had boldly committed early on.

A couple of years later, when Apple reinvented the rules of mobile communications with the iPhone, rather than becoming redundant, Samsung was the only incumbent manufacturer with the responsiveness to step up and compete. There, as elsewhere, the ride hasn't always been smooth and the roads taken haven't always worked out, but the company-wide motivational power of *muhantamgu* has ultimately taken it where it needed to go.

During its rise in the digital era, the company's organisation remained old-fashioned in many ways, however. It retained the same arcane top-down management structure, and its no-nonsense industrial-age ethos meant it was slow to incorporate marketing into its thinking. Then, when it belatedly sought out creative input from overseas, foreign talent often found the Samsung culture a difficult one to adapt to. Some of these old issues endure in the firm's approach even now, but, as it always did, Samsung's will to reach the required destination means the potholes are safely passed, the new routes eventually discovered.

If the company continues to succeed in the years to come, it will be because it has once again worked out how to instil its founder's infinite quest of 'endless striving' into the people who work for it.

Flexing towards the future

THE ACHIEVEMENTS OF Nike, Netflix, Disney, Pixar and Samsung clearly illustrate how today's most resilient creative businesses have been constructed so that disciplined productivity and free creativity are parts of a single, easily understood organisational ethos. They are examples of how the sum of the parts can be greater than the whole.

'Bureaucracy' has long been a dirty word in entrepreneurial circles. For most people in management today, the term signifies an organisation that moves at a plodding place and a system that's preoccupied with itself rather than its objectives. So, according to conventional wisdom, bureaucracy is the opposite of dynamic business practice. Yet a degree of bureaucratisation is most decidedly a necessity, and as such is not universally a bad thing. Properly applied, the word 'bureaucracy' simply describes the process of setting procedures for simple tasks that an organisation has to perform repeatedly – in other words, it means building a more efficient company.

Bureaucracy has been no less important to these twenty-first century success stories than it was to the great businesses of old; what matters is that the nature of effective bureaucratisation has evolved. The best companies now let their computers do it for them, so that their 'human resources', that is, people, can concentrate on being creative.

Building a system that engages instead of alienates its people; that corrects, rather than consolidates, its inbuilt errors; that gives people the right kind of sense of security without the wrong kind of sense of complacency: that's what all the successful businesses and leaders we've looked into in this chapter have striven for.

You don't have to embrace the mystical mandala to find a model. Nike is a vivid reminder of how the mould of professional athletes, who mix up their targets and routines whenever they feel things are getting too close to the comfort zone, can and should continually renew and re-energise an established organisation.

embrace the latest innovations, while harking back to the oldest human principles of order and harmony.

It's no coincidence that Nike, Netflix, Pixar and Samsung all saw, and committed to, the potential of digital very early on. Their decisive entries into their respective markets enabled them to do two positive things before their rivals. Firstly, they relocated their bureaucracies – their standardised, often-repeated tasks – into the market-leading software they built. A good algorithm is a piece of positive bureaucracy: it lets you outsource the lighting on an animated leaf, or the processing of a customer's past rentals into future recommendations, without human labour.

This outsourcing made possible their second positive response to digital change: it enabled them to recruit small, dedicated, well-rewarded workforces. Because such workers understand their role in the business and their vital contribution to its success, they typically stay loyal to a company and help it grow.

building a system that engages instead of alienates its people; that corrects, rather than consolidates, its inbuilt errors; that gives people the right kind of sense of security without the wrong kind of sense of complacency: that's what all the successful businesses and leaders we've looked into in this chapter have striven for.

When you take away unnecessary rules and mindless rituals, systems exist to ensure deadlines are met while quality standards are maintained. Every great business with aspirations to innovation and creativity has to ensure human frailty is accommodated and human brilliance is enabled. Preventing things from going wrong is important, but making sure people have room to do the most effective thing is just as vital. The rules these exemplary companies do retain are there to nurture, rather than police or stifle, their employees. The structures and systems they abide by simply ingrain a holistic sense of respect and responsibility.

All great organisations find their own unique ways to manage the inevitable tensions that arise between art and commerce, and punctuality and perfectionism. They put the friction these clashes cause to positive effect. These companies embrace the latest innovations, while harking back to the oldest human principles of order and harmony. They work out how to stop 'organisation' being a dreaded idea. That's why we should look to their examples – and why the first thing we should learn from those examples is that, if you want to get big but stay true to you, you have to find your own way to get it right.

Author

We make sense of life through stories. Told with sincerity, style and authority, an authentic story instantly resonates with the emotions of your audience.

Those Who Change Culture *are* Masters *of* Their Own Tales

THIS BOOK IS predicated on the principle that telling stories – that most basic and ancient of human habits – is what really lasts in our culture. Empires rise and fall, nations and corporations soar and sink, but the best stories never die.

Our shiny new digital economy has made old-fashioned talk of the importance of the story more important than ever. From professional sports to Michelin-starred restaurants, storytelling is explicitly acknowledged in all spheres of public life as a force that gives meaning to human experience and has a real impact on what individuals and communities can accomplish. At AKQA, we have always talked about 'telling stories through software' to convey our feeling that digital experiences are only memorable if they're given shape, structure and emotional resonance through narrational techniques. Recent bestselling popular science books on psychology, memory and anthropology by the likes of Daniel Kahneman (*Thinking, Fast And Slow*) and Yuval Noah Harari (*Sapiens: A Brief History of Humankind*) have used the latest science to illuminate the ways in which story is the fundamental form in which humans navigate and make sense of the world.

there may be security in settling for the comfort of being carried along by others' narratives, but there's no leadership in it.

Superficially, many leaders and organisations appear to acknowledge all this primal power; it's not just in Hollywood that lip service is always paid to story these days. Politicians talk about winning elections – even wars – in terms of disseminating 'the right narrative'. PR firms seek to 'control the story'. Many business leaders routinely talk in similar terms, but only a select few manage to go beyond routine storytelling. Most companies, the screenwriting guru Robert McKee once told the *Harvard Business Review*, prefer to present 'a rosy – and boring – picture to the world' rather than risk sharing the true drama and details of their success.

Those entrepreneurs and leaders who have most boldly and profitably harnessed the power of story have built their success on something even more impressive. The heroes of this chapter told their stories and then, through their business endeavours, made them come true. They used their respect for and love of storytelling, whether sartorial, cinematic or literary, to become authors of their own destinies.

It was only in the twentieth century that the word 'author' came to be understood as 'person who writes books'. Before that, it was used in English to mean an originating *authority* – i.e., someone who has claim to ownership or dominion over something. Even earlier than that, it also meant someone who laid claim to the promotion of something, which is why the word 'auctioneer' has the same Latin root as 'author'. But to make sense of the great authors of our business age, it's easier to look at a more familiar modern word: to 'authorise'. A law or a permit is just some words on a piece of paper or parchment until it's authorised, at which point it becomes a fact of life.

Author. Authenticity. Authority.

THE TALES TOLD in this chapter are of leaders who harness this authorial understanding to transform their worlds and workplaces. They know the stories they want to tell – because they love them and believe in them – and they keep their audiences enthralled. At the same time they have not stretched their brands beyond their natural (authentic) limits. And they do not worry about the short-term; Ralph Lauren built an $8-billion-a-year global empire out of story by upgrading the American dream and building a retail empire out of his teenage fantasies. Jeff Bezos makes the stripped-down, anti-glamour environment of the Amazon workplace into a galleon on the high seas through the power of story. And Joss Whedon and J.J.

Abrams weave their childhood love of stories into state-of-the-art reimaginings of popular culture classics expertly tailored to modern audiences and media formats. Story nourished them in their youths, then became their meal ticket and their route to greatness in adulthood.

We're genetically programmed to make sense of our lives by shaping our experience into story form. We can't do much about that. What we can do, if we have the capacity and the drive, is to prevent our story being dictated by others by telling a better one ourselves. When you look at it that way, good storytelling is entrepreneurship in a nutshell. There may be security in settling for the comfort of being carried along by others' narratives, but there's no leadership in it. Take control, claim authorship, tell a great tale, and the opportunities to build something real and lasting out of it are dazzling.

If you borrow a twist or two along the way from your inspirations, don't apologise; just make sure you make what you take your own. It's what the smartest storytellers have been doing all along.

Ralph Lauren:

Action is Character

THERE ARE TWO twentieth-century rags-to-riches stories whose power remains undimmed in our time. They're both tales of self-made men who changed their names, shaped their own myths and reinvented their identities. They depict American dreamers who made their fantasies of themselves and their fabulous lives into realities.

One, the fictional story of James Gatz, a man who transformed himself into 'The Great Gatsby', was first published 90 years ago, but people have felt compelled to retell it ever since – on stage and film from the days of silent screen to the age of digital 3D cinema. In the book, James Gatz's business success is shrouded in mystery, and the life he leads as Jay Gatsby ultimately ends in tragedy.

The second story, in contrast, is the true tale of Ralph Lifshitz. His business is his life, and the life he leads as Ralph Lauren is his triumph. His story endures because it too expresses and empathises with the universal desire for glamour and romance. As a person and a business leader, he's succeeded by giving his dreams material form, by realising his imaginary world until it was a fact, and then letting other people buy into it, one product at a time.

Ties that bind

AN UNDERSTANDING OF visual storytelling and sartorial symbolism came early to young Ralph – perhaps because he understood early that it was his best shot at being somebody. Born in the rough and rugged Bronx in 1939, the son of immigrants from Belarus, the slender, slightly built Ralph Lifshitz didn't have the easy athletic prowess or social assurance of his older brothers. A speech impediment that he struggled with at school made him more of a watcher than a talker, so he had to find other ways to communicate his vision of the person he wanted to be perceived as. At 16, tired of being teased about his surname, he boldly changed it to 'Lauren'. Though he was still very young, his confidence in the change came from his understanding of who he wanted to be – a confidence that was already evident in the way he wore his clothes and did his hair.

From his early teens onwards, Ralph's attention to and innate understanding of the unwritten codes of menswear enabled him to use his clothing to obtain the markers of status that fate had so far denied him. He wasn't the leader in track events or debating clubs, but he would be in charge when he accompanied his brothers and cousins on expeditions to second-hand clothing stores. There, Ralph's expertise in pivotal particulars would enable the boys to acquire the precise look of the private-school kids they so admired. Lauren's parents lacked the financial means to give their son the privileged life to which he aspired, but his foraging instincts and astute fashion sense enabled Ralph to assume the look that went with it – and for a fraction of the price.

the real question was whether or not you felt a connection to the sensibility that the outfits inspired by those pastimes evoked, and whether you too wanted to be a part of the tale they told and the world they made manifest.

The pronounced, self-possessed sense of style, and the confidence with which Ralph wore his unusual outfits, soon gave him an aura all of his own. From his mid-teens, he spent summers the same way his brothers had, as a supervisor at a summer camp. That expanded his social circle far beyond the limits of his Bronx-bound childhood, and enhanced his uptown ambitions still further.

It would be some while before Lauren's financial fortunes caught up with his fine taste and obsession with quality, but he tried to emulate the wealthy lifestyle as much as he could. In his early twenties, while doing sales jobs for stuffy men's clothiers like Brooks Brothers, he rented a relatively upscale apartment, bought Gucci gear and drove round in a flashy imported English convertible.

EVERYONE WHO EMPLOYED him in the early days, or even just sold him a tailor-made suit, couldn't help but sense that he was something special. The tailors, buyers and store managers who first worked with the young Lauren saw how his own retro-inflected sense of men's style, combined with the fastidiousness he'd inherited from his house-proud mother, meant he could arrange store displays and put together outfits like nobody else. Although his impressive confidence in his vision also made him a handful to deal with; whether buying or selling clothes, Ralph's insistence that everything had to be *just right* and nothing less often made life hard for his early mentors.

make the choice to step into the world of my dreams, and I'll make you feel a part of it.

In 1967 Ralph Lauren designed and produced the first Polo products: a small line of unusually wide ties in stunning fabrics, which were distributed by Beau Brummell, the neckwear firm for which he then worked as a salesman. By this time, fashion was already established as a newsworthy subject and a matter of cultural import. The arrival of machine-sewn, ready-to-wear designer fashion had established fashion's renewed media currency earlier in the decade. Now, in the year of 'the summer of love', increasingly outrageous rock-star looks and hair were morphing into beaded, tie-dyed hippie styles, augmented by elements of revolutionary chic.

Ralph Lauren's vision was of something less overtly attention-seeking, but altogether more enduring – namely a 'gentleman of distinction'. A person whose clothes suggested good breeding, rare education, refinement and a Gatsby-like capacity for the perfect gesture for any occasion.

As a great student of leading men in the movies, Lauren knew that, in menswear, it was the little details that marked the difference between being a star and being just another 'suit': details like the width of a lapel, the weight of a yarn, the curve of a shirt collar, the pop of a pocket square. The first step towards becoming 'distinguished' is to obsess over the little details about which most mere mortals are oblivious and only those in the know will ever notice.

The basics of men's clothing, as we still know them today, were first formalised in the nineteenth century. The shirts, jackets and slacks that defined twentieth century 'smartness' were all based on blocks and patterns that had been first introduced to create cultures of uniformity. The clothing of the Quakers, whose ethos stressed equality and shunned hierarchy, was one foundation; the growth of modern military forces, and the need to create durable, functional outfits for them, was the other. The singular codes that set elites apart, the textures that distinguish dapper dandies from drab salary-men, are rooted in the finer details of cut, feel, finish and styling – of the way a garment is worn and accessorised.

In for the long haul

THE WIDE TIES that became Lauren's Polo line were a case in point. For ages, he had badgered bosses and partners to produce wider ties, like the newly fashionable 'Kipper' ties from swinging London. When they finally let him make his own, his Beau Brummell superiors baulked at the cost of the luxurious fabric in outsized dimensions and rued his insistence on championing them more passionately than all their other products in his role as a salesman. But within a few months of their launch, the Polo ties became a sensation, landing Lauren his first media profiles and his first distribution deal with Bloomingdales.

As a boy from the hardscrabble Bronx, it goes without saying that Ralph Lauren's childhood world had little overlap with the upper-class sport of polo. He hadn't even ridden a horse before. But he was more than happy to clamber onto a pony, don a cap and wield a polo hammer for the brand's first-ever publicity shots. It was Lauren's first picture-perfect Polo moment – the story of a whole lifestyle captured in a single frame. In fact, it's no accident that Ralph Lauren all but invented the lucrative concept of the 'lifestyle brand': of the fashion label that convinces you it's not merely textiles or clothing, but components of a more elegant way of life.

As his company grew from those first ties, its ever-expanding range of lines eventually embraced every kind of high-class sport, tradition and pastime. At the same time, Ralph Lauren always managed to innovate in the way his brand communicated these noble pursuits. The issue was never about whether or not you actually went to a genuine preppie school, were a member of an Ivy League club or knew how to ride a horse. The real question was whether or not you felt a connection to the sensibility that the outfits inspired by those pastimes evoked, and whether you too wanted to be a part of the tale they told and the world they made manifest. Riffing on the symbols of high-born American tradition, the embroidered man on the horse was a powerful marker that you'd made it.

when leaders harness the full potential of story, and believe in its transformative powers themselves, they have the opportunity to shoot for a kind of immortality, building inimitable brands that refuse to fade.

Before Polo and the wealth that came with it, Ralph and his brothers were fashion freaks trying to look as distinguished as they could. Ralph would rummage through flea markets, admiring the thick weave of old English blazers, the cut of old military jackets, the beautiful stitching on pockets – all details that were absent from the new, machine-made clothes in the windows of Manhattan's fanciest stores. 'Curation', a word you now hear in modern fashion all the time, was very much what Ralph had been about from the beginning.

For the past few years, most high-end men's fashion has worked on the basis of a similar understanding. Brand emissaries are sent to select stalls in secret flea markets to hand over bundles of notes for ancient army-issue raincoats. Teams from Milan are dispatched to bring back inspiration from the vintage vendors of Pasadena. Crack squads of fashionistas go to buy up old couture collections for future inspiration, and the great brands constantly revisit their own archives for inspiration. That's why the men in the world's hipster hotspots tend to look like lumberjacks, 1950s mountain climbers, nineteenth-century Viennese intellectuals – or just plain preppies. 'Heritage', 'workwear' and 'vintage' are twenty-first century terms for the way clothing with stories to tell can confer mystique, character and substance on the men who wear them. They're all ways of expressing what Ralph Lauren has known for over half a century.

Lauren's appreciation of menswear's past and his demand for quality means his design process has always been rooted in visual reference and trial and error with texture. From the beginning, he'd go through endless looks or swatches of fabric, or boxes of old photos, until he found the right match for the mood he had in his head. However, although Lauren was always quick to point out when something *wasn't* right – when it wasn't 'Ralph Lauren' –

he was not always the most precise about articulating what he *did* want. For that reason, by the dawn of the 1980s, the company had a small army of experts and advisors who had learned to take a few quiet words or a singular picture from the great man and understand the entire scenario he wanted to evoke. They understood because they too believed; Lauren's values were theirs too, and his dream world was one into which they had been invited.

Joseph Abboud was one of the many designers who cut his teeth at Ralph Lauren before becoming a fashion name in his own right. 'Ralph was our hero,' he said of his time at Polo. 'We believed the myth; we dressed the myth. We were the legions. It was all-consuming, and we were sucked into it. It was a beautiful place to be.'

Kristin Holby was a model in many of the landmark campaigns legendary photographer Bruce Weber shot for Lauren in the 1980s, and she fondly remembers how comprehensive and contagious his world creation was:

It was the Ralph girl with her boyfriend, her sisters and her father-in-law. A cast of hundreds, men, women, children, animals. Twenty models paid to sit around, caviar served to us on the beach, no other client had a budget like that. They treated us like princes and princesses because they wanted us to feel wealthy. That's how they created the romance of it.

Lauren was offering a promise – that's why he always felt much more strongly about the importance of getting the perfect fabric than he did about staying on budget. He didn't only extend this aura of romance to his team of design assistants, his legions of models and extras; it was also part of the relationship he built with his customers: *Make the choice to step into the world of my dreams, and I'll make you feel a part of it.*

The customer service in the company's flagship stores is quite something. You get your own Gatsby moment as you find yourself being offered a drink that is beautifully served by a butler wearing white, and all the 'associates' (who might more prosaically be labelled 'sales people') have business cards they present you with in case of any follow-up questions. You feel they've invested effort in making you a part of the Lauren lifestyle before you've spent a dime.

an understanding of visual storytelling and sartorial symbolism came early to young Ralph – perhaps because he understood early that it was his best shot at being somebody.

Which, of course, only ensures that people do spend, and not just on clothes. Ralph Lauren remains the only brand to have forged a front-rank presence in both fashion and interiors, and you'll find his 'Home' products everywhere, including five-star hotels the world over. It feels like the right match, just as it's a perfect fit when he designs the suits for the US Olympic team or The All-England Tennis Club at Wimbledon. And Ralph Lauren Home (which celebrated its thirtieth anniversary in 2013) is just one of the family of over 20 distinct lines and sub-brands, catering to every age and aspect of life and work, that operate within the Ralph Lauren Corporation.

The American dreamer

KARL LAGERFELD ONCE said, 'Ralph gave American fashion a global image. He is the perfect illustration of the American dream.' It's not a new idea, but it is an important one in understanding Lauren's inimitable brand and unfaltering sense for a story that feels real.

It's the elusive American dream of a perfect existence, of a romantic ideal realised, that F. Scott Fitzgerald celebrates at the end of *The Great Gatsby*:

> Gatsby believed in the green light, the orgastic future that year by year recedes before us. It eluded us then, but that's no matter – tomorrow we will run faster, stretch out our arms further ... And one fine morning –
>
> So we beat on, boats against the current, borne back ceaselessly into the past.

A hero to the novel's narrator, Nick Carraway, Gatsby is a man 'worth the whole damn bunch put together' because he never surrenders his romantic hopefulness; he never dilutes or disconnects with his vivid dreams.

Ralph Lauren also believes in the green light too – in the power of dreams to become realities. Lauren himself has said time and time again that his greatest achievement is that there's no gap between brand and man, collections and creator, the reality and the dream.

Lauren's life, and that of the company he founded, demonstrated the validity of his proposition: if you dress like it, and do it with conviction, you *become* it. He wasn't simply selling a dream. Rather than something quantifiable, he was sharing a dream that was all-important to him at a deeply personal level.

And the beauty of Ralph's story is, unlike the Great Gatsby, he never tried to hide who he'd been to protect the image of who he'd become. Though still one more inclined to communicate with visuals rather than words, he has freely admitted that, as a boy, he'd envy his school-friends' grand homes, their opportunities ... even their shoehorns:

I was always into clothes, but I didn't have the money to buy them. When I'd get my brothers' hand-me-downs, there was an energy in me that made me say, 'I want to get my own things, to make my own statement.' Somewhere along the line, that energy – coupled with my exposure, through movies, to a world I hadn't known – turned into something.

The movie fan became the leading man. The painter's son became the preppy style legend. The fantasy became the facts. When leaders harness the full potential of story, and believe in its transformative powers themselves, they have the opportunity to shoot for a kind of immortality, building inimitable brands that refuse to fade.

Jeff Bezos & the Great Amazon Adventure

THOUGH HE'S USUALLY regarded as the single greatest disruptor of the traditional book-publishing business, Jeff Bezos has a deep and informed respect for the power of a well-wrought story. It's the Bezos mastery of story that makes his company's relentless chase for new markets, margins and methods feel like a quest rather than a drudge. It turns warehousing into an opportunity to create wonderment; office life into an odyssey.

The story Bezos has always told about the ultimate aim, the eternal goal that powered every single Amazon initiative wasn't some mythical goal, it was quite simply, the satisfaction of the Amazon customer. The adventure was how to get there.

This incredibly simple, old-fashioned idea, the one that underlies all business propositions, has been of immeasurable importance in shaping Amazon's spirit. Bezos often talks about the innovation 'spectrum' – the fact that it's just as important to make small, daily, incremental changes to how you work as it is to launch expensive new projects. It's one of the many ways in which Amazon's grand technological and commercial vision is tempered by a rare awareness of human scale. The MayDay feature for the Amazon Kindle Fire introduced video-chat direct with a sales representative. Aptly named for the old nautical SOS term, MayDay connected organisational brilliance, technological audacity and an intimate understanding of what it takes to make people's lives better.

Though his company's achievements in data collection, storage and analysis are legion, they all stem from Bezos's ability to articulate Amazon's aims in clear narrative form. The intended destination of each quest never changes – it's the customer. But because Amazon likes to travel into what Bezos calls 'unknown geographies', the correct route to that goal can never be accurately mapped in advance. The way Bezos tells it, this is part of the satisfaction of pursuing new frontiers. By weaving a story of adventure into the fabric of Amazon's daily practice, he elevates limitations into challenges and defeats into lessons.

This conviction about leadership as authorship, in the power of narrative to give shape and purpose to a workforce, gave Bezos the confidence to forego the act of spinning different yarns for different audiences. Instead, everyone – customers, coders, employees and investors alike – get to hear the same story. They might not always like what they're told, but if they have faith in Amazon and its leadership, they're generally willing to stay on board until they hear the next chapter.

The adventure story Bezos inculcates into the people he employs at Amazon isn't a made-up fable. The true essence of the mission, to cut the number of steps between producer and consumer, whatever it takes, lies at the heart of the stories he tells, just as it defines his company's greatest achievements. From cutting wasteful journeys and packaging to enabling authors to upload books direct to the Kindles in their fans' hands to being able to speak your every need into an always-listening shopping robot, Amazon's market-changing innovations have always been the ones that further this quest. (And, whether because of clunky interfaces or excessive interstitial promotions for Amazon services, the ones that fail most painfully tend to be the ones that stray from it.)

'adventure' means taking a journey whose route is unmapped, and embracing the goal of a destination, while accepting that there are no guarantees you'll get there. In business terms, adventure is about combining a naïve, childlike appetite for the new and the imaginative with a mature, grown-up capacity for resilience, patience, disappointment and even failure.

Private customers anticipate evermore innovations to bring them more of what they want – quicker, easier and sooner. A similar ethic holds for Amazon's massive range of business customers, in everything from fulfilment to data storage. But the people charged with playing the leading roles in Amazon – the workers and shareholders alike – are told to wait for the ending rather than insist on quarterly dividends, or insist on instant enlightenment along the way. That adventure story, and Bezos's confidence in telling it, is what has always kept doubters on board when the waters seemed choppy.

As Bezos once told the *New York Times*:

> We are willing to think long term. We start with the customer and work backwards. And, very importantly, we are willing to be misunderstood for long periods of time.

When an ending's worth shooting for, it's worth waiting for.

Two men in a boat

THE FIRST PERSON Bezos converted to his spirit of adventure was his first employee, Shel Kaphan. Kaphan had taught himself code and planned to launch his own startup in the 1990s, until he met Bezos. The adventure Bezos promised him, of a quest to bring one of a million books to any door, resonated with Kaphan. Kaphan was a child of the 1960s who had interned at the *Whole Earth Catalog* – subtitled 'Access to Tools' – in his teens, and he saw books as a crucial tool that Bezos aimed to bring to every home.

Kaphan lived in Santa Cruz, California, at the time of the company's foundation. When he started work in

Bezos's Bellevue garage in 1994, the nascent business was going by the name 'Cadabra', and he had to go out and buy its first computers. Little literature about coding for the web existed then, and established database systems were patchy and incompatible. Kaphan was excited by the challenge of creating a new kind of online environment. Next, if he wanted to stay on board the journey, he had to embrace Bezos's adventuring urges and leave his home for a new kind of physical environment too.

One of the reasons Bezos decided books would be the first thing Amazon sold was that they could be posted cost-effectively and with minimal packaging. Having made this typically acute decision, he decided that destination also meant that he and his young company should move to Seattle. It may have been far from home, and far from the glamorous Californian bases of other dot.com darlings, but, with the destination set, it was the best choice if the company was to deliver. This was for three reasons: Seattle was the home of one of the country's major book distributors, it had a relatively low rate of sales tax and it had lots of skilled workers in the areas Amazon needed.

Kaphan came along, came up with the name 'Amazon' and continued with the ride for a five further years. When he left, he couldn't have imagined the areas Amazon would reach into over the next 15 years. The narrative drive to adventure was key to all of them. Consider the Amazon data and storage spin-off Amazon Web Services. Its clients include millions of businesses and many thousands of government institutions around the world. It's trusted, it's easy to use and it's communicated to people in clear, actionable terms.

This success can be traced back to Bezos's original leadership on the project. In 2002, frustrated at a lack of progress and failures of internal communication of the nascent project, he wrote out a simple, six-bullet story intended to bridge the gap between his horizons and those of his coders, and get everybody pulling together. Even though it was a plain-English action plan for a job rooted in rich and complex systems of numbers, it transformed the project and the company. Today, Bezos always insists that an old-fashioned written 'narrative' precedes any major new coding project, to ensure the clever numbers people don't lose their way.

it's the Bezos mastery of story that makes his company's relentless chase for new markets, margins and methods feel like a quest rather than a drudge.

To its customers, Amazon is the ultimate stay-at-home convenience: a service that delivers everything they need to their doorstep, their office desk or their mobile phone screen. But for its employees, who are expected to show endurance and endeavour at all times, the essence of Amazon is Bezos's spirit of adventure, and the way it filters down to all who fly under his flag.

That may seem a hyperbolic description of a logistics company devoted to taking the hassle out of shopping, but it's actually the simple, sober truth about the brilliance of Bezos. 'We have an explorer mentality,' he has often said, 'so we like to go pioneering.' Properly used, 'adventure' means taking a journey whose route is unmapped, and embracing the goal of a destination, while accepting that there are no guarantees you'll get there. In business terms, adventure is about combining a naïve, childlike appetite for the new and the imaginative with a mature, grown-up capacity for resilience, patience, disappointment and even failure.

Risk and reward

BEZOS REGARDS THE spirit of adventure as a necessity, and sees the failures along the way as the proof that you are embracing that spirit fully. To embrace adventure is to embrace risk – especially when you believe, as Bezos does, that the greatest risk to the future of a firm is when it conservatively tries to avoid risk altogether. As he told the audience at a conference in New York late in 2014:

> I've made billions of dollars of failures at Amazon.com. Literally billions … Companies that don't embrace failure and continue to experiment eventually get in the desperate position where the only thing they can do is make a Hail Mary bet at the end of their corporate existence.

As a leader with that belief about business, he added, 'My job is to encourage people to be bold.' That encouragement does not come in the way of perks or idle flattery; Bezos is famously direct in his criticism, but always directional too. At other celebrated companies, symbols of status or/and wealth inevitably seem to sprout from financial success and handsome share options. At Amazon, Bezos's story-telling chops have enabled him to build a company where the most aspirational idea of all is still what it always was: to economise. To save money in the name of the cause, not splash it on fripperies.

By sticking to the adventure story, Bezos joins up the countless component parts of his business into aspects of one single, unambiguous mission. Bezos once told *Forbes* magazine:

> Full sentences are harder to write. They have verbs. The paragraphs have topic sentences. There is no way to write a six-page, narratively structured memo and not have clear thinking.

Early in its evolution, consumers saw Amazon as an organisation whose closest competitors were bookstore chains like Barnes & Noble. Today, the company has ventured out into so many areas, it's ridiculous to try to pin down any one entity as its chief rival: Wal-Mart? Netflix? Target? Apple? When you consistently go as big, as broadly and as boldly into all-new territories as Amazon does, you leave the very possibility of a comprehensive competitor in your wake. And because the organisation keeps on expanding with an adventurous ethos – a goal that no mists along the way can obscure – the difference between Amazon's footprint and the combined efforts of the rest just keeps growing.

An obvious example of this exponential effect of Amazon's adventurousness is 'Weblab', the company's 'internal experimentation' platform, which is used to assess and explore improvements to the company's products and services. There were 546 Weblab experiments in 2011, 1,092 in 2012 and by 2013 no fewer than 1,976. One great case study is the 'frustration-free packaging' initiative Amazon launched in collaboration with major brands including Mattel and Unilever. A decade on, Amazon was asking why so many other products still had such lavishly excessive boxes. By the end of 2013, Amazon had signed up 2,000 brands to the programme, and sent the new improved packaging to 213 countries, saving 15 million kilos' worth of packing waste in the process. With numbers like those, Bezos can always show the tireless explorers who work for him that their efforts are not in vain.

There are plenty more numbers, of course: Amazon's bots go out exploring every night, and come back to correct any of their prices being undercut on the web. Amazon's forays into such diverse fields as digital hardware, film and TV content creation, fresh food and high fashion have come thick and fast, generating impressive growth in the process.

But the numbers alone aren't what turn the Amazon worker's seemingly ordinary world of brown boxes, returns labels, call centres and enormous warehouses into the base-camps for an epic adventure. Amazon may act on and interpret its data with lightning speed and efficiency, but it's those inspirational words that tie the entire grand project together.

Notwithstanding his critics in the old bricks-and-mortar book trade, Jeff Bezos is, among many other things, an ardent lover of literature. He spent $280 million on the struggling *Washington Post*, a move that shocked many neophyte digital types, and then bolstered its editorial staff as well as its digital resources, leading to new apps and services and a huge increase in online readership. He's also married to a novelist. There's no denying his commitment to the survival of the story.

The incredible journey

AS WITH HIS employees, Jeff Bezos championed the adventure narrative – the promise of privations, tough times and exhilarating triumphs to come – from the very first page of the Amazon story. At the end of 1997, in his first-ever letter to Amazon shareholders, he explained how he always told interviewees, 'You can work long, hard or smart, but at Amazon.com, you can't choose two out of three.' He didn't want people who wanted a job. He wanted people who wanted to work at Amazon. Salaries were competitive but not excessive, because share options were a better way to breed long-term commitment and an in-the-round approach to the company's success. Cost-efficiency always came before comfort for comfort's sake. Bezos asked employees to think of the company's money as their own.

This message – that to succeed at adventuring, you should cautiously preserve your resources until you really need them for the unforeseen challenges to come – was the one investors heard too. Sceptical analysts have long criticised Amazon's small margins and its low rate of profit to revenue, but, with his destination always on his mind, Bezos has never changed path. If the company reinvests in providing a quicker and better service to its customers – whether in the form of discounts, new depots, two-hour delivery trial schemes, airborne delivery drones, to unprecedented arrangements with the United States Postal Service to distribute its packages on Sundays – then eventually, the reach of the business will mean that those who stayed the course will get their reward.

At a 2011 Amazon shareholders' meeting, Jeff Bezos was asked, since there were no huge write-offs or missteps that year, whether the company was becoming overly cautious in its adventuring. 'In a way,' Bezos replied, 'That is, like, the nicest compliment I'd ever had.' They'd had a lucky run, he said, and there *would* yet be costly failures to come, but he also felt that the data he and his colleagues gathered on their early adventures was now leaving them better equipped to navigate new territory. 'We know how to open new geographies,' he said. 'That doesn't mean these things are guaranteed to work, but we have a lot of expertise and knowledge.'

connected organisational brilliance, technological audacity and an intimate understanding of what it takes to make people's lives better.

He was right about the failures too; among the many successful Amazon adventures embarked on since, some, such as the Fire phone, have been very expensive experiments. But the bigger news has been much better. In January 2015, after a year of disappointing profits, Amazon rewarded its investors with 45 cents earnings per share – more than twice what the market had anticipated – and a swaggering last-quarter profit of $214 million. Bezos also revealed to shareholders that global membership of Amazon Prime had increased by 53 per cent year-on-year. Amazon also had the numbers to prove that Prime customers – whose annual subscriptions get them a year of no-cost next-day deliveries and other benefits – spent much more on the site on each year than the average user. As Amazon's customers increasingly embraced the opportunity to pay a one-off fee to accelerate their deliveries, its loyal investors congratulated themselves on having heeded Jeff's wisdom and waited when share prices had dipped. By committing to the long-haul voyage, they too got their rewards in the end.

Joss Whedon, J.J. Abrams and the 1,001 Stories

STORIES BREED STORIES. One generation of storytellers influences the next, and shapes the stories they tell. The more stories you are exposed to, the better equipped you are to create your own that win new audiences by tapping into age-old emotions. The reasons we keep coming back to the same images and archetypes is because they resonate with us on a fundamental level. That's not plagiarism – that's the whole point. Story wins. In recent years, you haven't had to browse the anthropology section of the library to see vivid examples of this; you've simply had to go to your local multiplex once in a while, or tune in to one of your smaller screens.

But this story begins with two boys, both born in New York City in the mid-1960s, into families of professional storytellers. Jeffrey Abrams's parents were television producers. Joseph Whedon's father was a screenwriter, just as his grandfather was before that, and his mother was a teacher who also wrote novels. Both boys also had siblings who went on to write for the screen. They learned early what it meant to try to make a living by telling stories, and they both decided early that, despite all the challenges and frustrations of the job, it was the one for them too.

Screenwriters-for-hire have traditionally been the bottom of the Hollywood food chain. Even well-rewarded, in-demand ones have to accept that their stories might never get made, or might be altered beyond all recognition when they finally reach the screen. Until a few years ago, television ranked low in the movie world's esteem too, with the small screen seen as a poor relation or runner's-up prize to the big. Though they both started out as writers, and both found fame through their work for TV, Abrams and Whedon have gone on to become the directors entrusted with steering the latest instalments of the most bankable movie blockbusters of the twenty-first century.

This reversal of fortune highlights how much the mechanics and methodology of the entertainment business has changed during the quarter-century over which Whedon and Abrams have been a part of it. What enabled both of them to make the most of those changes was an unflagging appetite for authoring new tales, and a relentless drive to use any means available to ensure that those tales got to reach their public.

Their stories weren't always the most popular, the most acclaimed or the most original – but their impulse to tell more stories, and find people who wanted to hear them, always carried them through the disappointments. Rather than wait, Cinderella-style, for the perfect director or deal to realise their vision, they took every opportunity to create and collaborate if it got their work out there. Like modern-day versions of Scheherazade, the heroine of the *One Thousand and One Nights*, who tells a thousand stories in succession to stay alive, they have told tales as though their lives depended on it. And they have always found a way to make their stories work – regardless of what money or media were made available to them to do it with.

This adaptability was a far cry from the classic twentieth-century authorial cliché of the tortured creator: the genius novelist or cinema auteur who works away in secrecy for years until every word or frame is in accord with their original vision. Instead, ahead of their time, Abrams and Whedon fitted the new paradigm for our time, intuiting what every brand or individual with an active social-media presence realised rather later: in the digital world, story is a volume business.

Before they reached their thirties, Whedon and Abrams had both managed to establish themselves as writers for the screen. When Abrams was just 25, the film of his screenplay *Regarding Henry* was released. Decidedly mixed reviews of the story couldn't dent the thrill of his childhood idol Harrison Ford taking the lead. Many critics disliked *Forever Young*, the Abrams-scripted movie that was released as a Mel Gibson vehicle the following year, but audiences disagreed; Abram's now-familiar storytelling mix of the domestic, the fantastical and the feel-good gave them everything they needed with their popcorn.

Joss Whedon is a couple of years older than J.J. Abrams, and by 1989, when friends roped a 23-year-old Abrams into penning his first feature, Whedon was already a valued writer for smash shows such as *Roseanne*. Soon, he flourished as a script doctor, spicing up bland screenplays with his talent for sharp, funny and stylish dialogue. He was a key member of the writing team on Pixar's first hit feature, *Toy Story*. As a screenwriter, he was enjoying an extraordinary start to his career. But he was still 'just' a screenwriter. It was what happened to one of his most cherished creations, and what he did about it, that set him on the path to being an author of such unprecedented impact.

Once more, with feeling

BEFORE HIS WORK on *Toy Story*, Whedon had sold a script called *Buffy the Vampire Slayer*. The campus-based story and its unlikely set-up had first taken shape in Whedon's mind while he was still a student. He was amused and inspired by the imaginative challenge of taking the staple elements of the pulp horror movies he loved, but turning them on their heads. In Whedon's genre saga, the archetypal blonde cheerleader, who was the ultimate objectified victim in most horror movies, would become the heroine. This inversion would enable him to find new angles on the primal fears and passions that scary stories tap into.

That was what he thought when he wrote the script, but the *Buffy* film that made it to the big screen in 1992 told a different story. Like so many screenwriters, Whedon saw his delight at his story being made turn to disappointment at what was made of it. Though it retained much of his peppy dialogue, the film robbed Whedon's Buffy lore of its nuance and darker depths and was a critical and commercial failure.

That might have been it, had Whedon not felt so insistently that Buffy's story still deserved to be told the right way. Less than five years later, Whedon got the opportunity to revisit the *Buffy* story as a pilot, then a series, for Fox TV. *Buffy the Vampire Slayer* was an unlikely proposition for its time – an effects-heavy fantasy show whose success would depend on audiences getting its meta-mentality, and in young adults as well as teens tuning in. But Fox, the youngest US TV network, had always been seen as something of an upstart, and it was still flush from the success of shattering received wisdom several years earlier – when it commissioned the half-hour primetime animation series *The Simpsons*.

Fox was willing to take a chance on Whedon. Whenever its executives *did* doubt the young writer, in the months over which the series was developed, and the years after, Whedon fought for control of everything: casting, direction, budget, writing. He wasn't going to let the essence of his story slip away a second time. Whedon stuck with the same essential story as the earlier failed film, but kept its integrity and original details intact. His faith in the value of his tale, when told properly, was to change television forever.

After just a few episodes, people got over *Buffy*'s seemingly inane premise – a cheerleader's struggle against vampires and werewolves – and spoke out about what a genre-defining show it was. It's hard to exaggerate the impact of its seven-series run on the wider television and movie scene too. Four years before the film sequences of *Lord of the Rings* and *Harry Potter* started in earnest, *Buffy* made it okay to admit you were a fantasy or sci-fi geek in public.

Two years after *Buffy* first aired, *The Sopranos* made its debut on HBO. People soon got over its core premise – a ruthless mobster sees a shrink and pours out his heart. That show, another often now cited as one of the very best ever, begot the era of the great HBO dramas and, later, the story-over-schedules successes of Netflix. Audiences appreciated the way these shows respected their intelligence. They saw how their many hours' running time, stretched over weekly episodes, allowed their characters to develop in ways no movie could match. They also liked the way that, once established, these programmes could pull off bold artistic feats in pacing or style – like 'Once More, With Feeling', the *Buffy* episode which, thanks to a spell, was entirely performed in song.

More directly, *Buffy*'s critical TV success and committed adult audience once again made the big screen a safe place for big-budget teenage vampires, boy wizards and games of thrones. Joss Whedon's series also foreshadowed J.J. Abrams's own small-screen successes: first the supernatural *Felicity* in 1998, then the hit crime-drama *Alias,* in which Jennifer Garner lacked occult powers, but was nevertheless very much a post-Buffy superhero in her role as a gadget-happy CIA agent.

Lost and found

BUT IT WAS with *Lost*, the series that first aired on ABC in 2004 and ran for six seasons, that Abrams's storytelling stamp became most clear, and his reputation as a distinct authorial force emerged. For a network TV show that depended on ratings for its survival, the brilliance of his approach was that he turned up the volume – not with special effects and shattering sounds but with the sheer quantity of story. In the show, with its vast cast of 20-plus leads, he honed his trademark: juggling and intertwining the stories and backstories of numerous characters so rapidly that not even the most attention-deficient audience could tune out. In J.J. Abrams's many worlds, as in his working life, there's simply no such thing as waiting around for something to happen.

Before any one *Lost* storyline ran out of steam or became remotely predictable, another two would artfully sprout in its place. Abrams is a Hydra of storytelling. That's why, regardless of its critics and faltering phases,

Lost kept so many millions of viewers hooked for so long with its suspense-stoking and picturesque red herrings. That's why, after making a decent directorial job of rebooting Tom Cruise and his *Mission Impossible* series in 2006, and producing big-screen breakthrough *Cloverfield* in 2008, Abrams was handed the reins to the second biggest classic sci-fi franchise on our planet: the one first re-imagined for the big screen when Abrams and Whedon were in their teens.

Abrams's new era *Star Trek* movies were massive box-office hits. Their space setting, with all its possibilities of time travel and beaming up, enabled the storyteller extraordinaire's imagination to run wild. His love for and knowledge of the original *Star Wars* movies was inescapably evident throughout – just as *Super 8*, made between the two *Star Treks* – was an homage to Spielberg's great breakthrough classics.

Joss Whedon always stays busy. Despite commercial disappointments with post-*Buffy* TV experiments, and even as it began to look as though he'd go down in posterity as The *Buffy* Guy, the ultimate niche hero, he kept on telling stories in every medium, including print comics, films and Internet TV shows. Then, in the past few years, the talent many had always sworn could some day take over Hollywood suddenly seemed to come out of nowhere to do just that. The impact of Whedon's hip horror *The Cabin in the Woods* abruptly repositioned him as the high-concept screenwriter of the moment when the other 2012 film he not only co-wrote, but also directed, became the biggest box-office success in the USA and around the globe that year. Based on the Marvel comic of the same name, *The Avengers* went on to become the third-highest grossing film of all time in North America.

In his writing and direction of *The Avengers*, Joss Whedon managed to combine the bubblegum of films like *Fantastic Four* with just a touch of the *Dark Knight*'s brooding seriousness. But mainly it was about lots of bright, entertaining bursts – precisely what everyone wanted from a gaggle of beloved old superheroes. Whedon's storytelling skills, honed on the small screen, meant that modish dramatic cutting was forsaken for coherent action, and sheer spectacle was never allowed to take over from pure storytelling.

It's at this point that the stories of Joss Whedon and J.J. Abrams overlap once again with that of Disney. After merging with Pixar, Disney had acquired two other giant entertainment brands. In 2009, Disney spent $4 billion to acquire Marvel Entertainment. Only a decade earlier, Marvel had gone through its own process of re-acquiring franchises it had sold off, turning forgotten characters into multimillion-dollar revenue sources and becoming a giant player even as the sales of comic books themselves dwindled.

Then in 2012, Disney bought Lucasfilm for a similar sum. In so doing, Disney became an entertainment conglomerate inconceivable when Whedon and Abrams wrote their first screenplays. Three great twentieth-century powerhouses of American popular storytelling were all part of one business. Disney was now also the home of the biggest sci-fi series ever and the most famous superheroes in comic book history, and its reach into family life went from toddlers to Star Wars-loving teens (and their parents). The huge, long-established marketing power of the space saga and the comic characters was now part of Disney's ecosystem of characters and creations, of cinema, television and theme parks. In 2013, it announced that J.J. Abrams would be directing an all-new *Star Wars* trilogy.

In one way, the new supercharged Disney is just another example of how stories have a way of coming round again. In his early days as a patron of special effects technology at Industrial Light & Magic – the visual effects company he founded – George Lucas had of course been the original incubator of the Pixar team. On the other hand, the friendly collision of these three lucrative pop cultural universes is likely to mean all kinds of new stories and overlapping products in years to come, told in formats and combinations we can't yet anticipate. With their capacity to keep on telling relevant stories regardless of the mutable demands of their environments, Abrams and Whedon could hardly be better placed to steer the planet's biggest franchises.

Audiences make authors

JOSS WHEDON AND J.J. Abrams know what it's like to be a fan. Rather than distance themselves from that world once they became leaders on the other side, both have taken pains to forge connections with their audiences throughout their careers. When everybody knows your television drama has made it through several seasons – thanks as much to vocal and influential fans as audience share – there's no reason to be shy about your ongoing gratitude.

The pair's natural inclination towards appreciative dialogue with their audience has proved a natural fit with the entertainment industry of our times. Today, once-niche fan events such as Comic-Con are now as vital to a blockbuster's PR schedule as any celebrity premiere. And production companies, such as Legendary Pictures look to fan bases to inspire their new ventures. Formed in 2000, Legendary has realised many modern comic-book adaptations, and a string of super-hits – from *300: Rise of an Empire* to *Godzilla* and *Interstellar* – on the basis of a novel and respectful monetisation of modern fan-base communities. (Legendary's founder Thomas Tull initially set up his company with an innovative investment strategy, convincing hedge-fund managers who normally steered clear of Hollywood that existing metrics about non-movie fandom – such as comics, conventions and online discussion – could be converted into predictors of box-office success.)

In the process of directing movies with his customary respect for schedules and budgets, Abrams made time to tell stories about their creation. While the original *Star*

Wars trilogy and George Lucas's prequels had been filmed in atmospheres of great secrecy, Abrams spent the new shoots sharing teasing glimpses of his cast and sets on Instagram. Aware of the impossibility of keeping everything under wraps in a smartphone world, he embraced authorship of the making-of gossip about his own movie. It's a typically astute move from this master storyteller – ever keen to move with the times rather than fight them.

Perhaps it's the apprenticeships that Abrams and Whedon served in the grounded, demanding, resource-constrained world of serial TV – where your audience figures determine whether you come back next season, or even next week – that sets them apart from the excesses of movie directors who went before them.

They are consummate modern authors, but they are absolutely not 'auteurs' in the fancy filmic sense. Working in the fantasy field and commissioning digital effects on tight budgets, they've always had to compromise and collaborate to realise their stories. They've always had to acknowledge their avid fans and to operate in a world where merchandising and commercial considerations have to be embraced by storytellers. Their model of authorship never presumes entitlement to an audience, but obliges them to go out and win one. Having grown up in television families, both men knew early that your stories only counted as long as people continued to gather to watch you tell them.

When you look at how the entertainment landscape has already changed over the working lives of Joss Whedon and J.J. Abrams, it's impossible to say that these masters of the cliffhanger won't yet go on to even more dramatic chapters yet. The billing may be bigger and better these days, and the level of control improved beyond all reckoning, but the story's still the thing.

If you don't want to be a
character in somebody else's story,
tell a better one yourself

THIS BOOK CHAMPIONS what we can learn from stories of business, but it's also about the business of storytelling. Back in the twentieth century, they used to say 'everybody has a novel in them'. Today – as well as opportunities for self-publishing aplenty – times have moved on, and we have countless readily accessible means and media for telling stories with. To assert your authorship in an assured and engaging way, you have to make the most of the tools around you to engage your audience. That's why J.J. Abrams, tweeting away to fans while working on the most anticipated movie saga in years, is such an apt example for our connected age.

Authorship is an instructive model for leadership because, once again, it is all about inspiring people, rather than bossing them about. For people to want to listen in the first place, your story has to compel people's attention. For them to stay with it, and for it to go on to stay with them, your story has to connect with their emotions and imagination. You can only become the author of your own business success with the permission of your audience.

New methods of storytelling breathe new life into familiar tales and stale old genres. Even if they're telling old stories, exceptional leaders always find a way to communicate what they're doing, and why they're doing it now, in their own distinct voices. Their authorial aptitude and confidence is what turns them from operations into emotions and from corporations into beloved brands. It's what makes their stories so singularly their own. Ralph Lauren made a thoroughly modern kind of company by celebrating a bygone golden age of style. Jeff Bezos steers his radical digital experimenters by talking like a seventeeth-century sea captain. Joss Whedon and J.J. Abrams told so many stories they earned the right to re-animate the pop-cultural properties of their youth.

Each of our authors had a prodigious sense of narrative direction – an unusually well-evolved, highly motivating sense of the kinds of stories they wanted to tell. That didn't mean they always knew what would happen next; it just meant that, when faced with the next unlikely plot twist or unexpected business development, they dealt with the challenge better than most. Their sense of story told them where to go next, without delay. It made them focus on being empathetic and entertaining. Every failed story presented an opportunity to enrich their understanding and improve their approach.

Whether you're starting a business or steering an old one into new waters, such a foundation of authorial authority is invaluable. If you've assembled a story that expresses your aims and values through terms and tropes that people want to listen to, and find it easy to make sense of, you have an enviable buttress against future shocks. What happens to the idea of the preppy hero, the rebel alliance, the art of home delivery when the next culture shock comes round the corner? If you believe in the tales you tell the world, you'll be ideally positioned to adapt them, and with them your whole business, when that world changes.

Those of us who've chosen to tell our stories in the field of business can leave the minutiae of narrative theory to the academics and aspiring screenwriters. It doesn't really matter whether you think there are only really three, five or seven basic plots in the world. The point is that worthwhile stories stay in our personal and cultural consciousness. Claiming authorship is about first acknowledging the basic, ancient power of story, then having enough creativity and command of the form to harness its power for your own ends.

That last part is the difference between an authoritative entrepreneur and just another storyteller. Though authorship doesn't have to be dependent upon originality, it *is* always about making the effort to transform your materials to your context, rather than copying and pasting them from the past. As any student of 1980s action movies will insist, the straight remakes are never as good as the originals.

Conclusion

Seek terrain unexplored

MORE OFTEN THAN not, when people tell you to 'know your limits', they're telling you to know your place. They're warning you not to get ideas above your station. But in this case, as with so many others, a shift in perspective can be transformative.

Knowing your limits – having the humility to accept that you operate within certain conventions and assumptions, and the courage and patience to try to work out what those boundaries are – might just be the foundation for going beyond them. If, like an athlete, you interrogate those limits to set a new personal best, then – as a person or as a business leader – you might just be in with a shot at bringing about worthwhile change in your life and your world.

The hamster wheel of grown-up life sometimes seems to drill this out of us, but '*why?*' is the most natural human question of all. It's the relentless refrain of the endlessly inquisitive young child, constantly exploring their potential in the physical world, at the same time as trying to make sense of the strange way adults do things. *But why does it have to be like that?*

Progress down the millennia has been the product of adults asking that very question, then getting to work putting it to the test. I don't know if the first human technologies were spears, tents or hammers, but I do know somebody had to make the mental leap of imagining each of them, and probably persisting through painful failed attempts, before they could become realities. If we are not brave enough to believe in the possibility of a slightly different world, we can only work within existing horizons and walk paths others have already worn down before us.

Because we can't have a guarantee about something that has never been tried before, optimism is vital to putting this pioneering spirit to practical use. It's the default starting position for Limitless leaders because it enables them to stake their faith and funds on the future that they want to make happen. When you have a deep-rooted conviction about doing something better, that faith is crucial for nourishing the daily drive, endurance and resilience it takes to see lasting change through.

Leading an organisation of any kind – a company, a team, a family – is hard. It's about constant sacrifice – sleep, leisure, money – in your own suddenly less-than-private life, offered in the safety-net-free hope of making that organisation succeed. Sometimes your compassion may clash with your hopes for the organisation's endurance; at other times, growing up and getting serious may endanger your ability to adapt, or make you too risk-averse to keep asking, '*But why ...?*'. Inevitably, creating a good organisation – creating anything good – entails grappling with these conundrums, never relaxing into the reassuring groove of letting your alert, aware attention fade into mere routine.

If you are able to keep vigilant about these things, and you have the right idea or product or service at the right time, and the right tools to see it through, the rewards can be immense. Pioneers get to make their mark over the frontiers they cross. People notice what improves their lives. They remember what matters. They want to feel optimistic too. If you get it right and then work to keep getting it right in new ways for changing times, your customers will continue to reward you.

The greatest leaders in business have all understood or intuited this, and their stories can help all of us be better because of it. They demonstrate that really thinking about what it means to truly democratise can lead to your influence reaching further than you can imagine. They remind us that to revolutionise in business, you not only have to have a vision; you also have to be able to bring others in to share it if you want to make it real. They show us that to simplify is to respect the way humble disciplines lay the foundations for unimaginable achievements. That to organise is to have an endless appetite for evolution, questioning convention so that creativity isn't stifled by growth. And that to author is to lay claim to your destiny and enthral your audience in a world shaped by story.

These insights have a certain warmth and a quiet wisdom about them. That's what makes what they have to share easier to relate to, and more meaningful than abstract or theoretical formulas for perfection.

Each story in this book focused on a leader who broke

through one or more barriers – technical, cultural, geographical – by the force of their openness and ability to back it up. While technological skills were crucial to the success of several of them, the capacity for expansive imagination always mattered more. The rest of us can't demolish the barriers those leaders tore down; the limits that they proved were illusory. But we can seek to break fresh ground of our own, equipped with the tools of the present.

During a planetary metamorphosis that is relentless, unforgiving, accelerating and unstoppable we all yearn for some kind of permanence and certainty. That's why there will always be more lasting value in the wisdom of all time, rather than the know-it-all assumptions of our own time.

If it's truly wise, the wisdom of the past is also the wisdom of the present. If you strip away the latest management jargon and tune out the hype on the latest start-up sensation, it's hard not to notice that the simple strengths which make for great leadership never rust or fade. The times, technologies and currencies will continue to change but essential truths about people, their dreams and their trials have not.

When I started to research my heroes for this book, in the hope that their wisdom might also be useful to others, I found that the stories of the leaders and companies I so admired were interconnected in ways I'd never imagined. That Sony's founder Akio Morita had been an admirer of Henry Ford. That Bill Gates helped create the building where Google was built. That Henry Ford had learned what not to do from the great Thomas Edison, and Coco Chanel mastered the elevation of the everyday object to design classic for the industrial age just as Steve Jobs would for the digital. Motifs from much older stories kept magically reappearing in newer ones. They remind us that even the most legendary, charismatic, high-achieving organisations had known doubt, despair and failure.

I hope each person who reads *Limitless* can draw new connections between these stories, and can find new ways to apply the principles that underlie them in their lives. That would be the best proof of their value as wisdom for the ages.

There's a kind of serenity to be found in pulling back from your immediate obsessions, passing panics and day-to-day business decisions; a calm to be drawn from the knowledge that 5 or 5,000 years before you, somebody faced far greater challenges – and came through them triumphantly. But, for me at least, it's not the kind of serenity that makes you want to retire to a remote location with a parasol and a yoga mat. On the contrary, I've found having a broader, longer-term understanding reinvigorates you for the next challenge.

It also does something far more important. Studying organisations from other eras promotes a sense of duty beyond the next set of results or the expectations of your shareholders. It instils a more expansive sense of your responsibility to the future, an understanding that the companies that make the most difference, and often the most profit, are the ones that were founded to pursue long-term aims, rather than short-term gains.

If you're able to get some perspective on your present-day challenges, chances are you'll see you're not as alone as you feel. Those who created great and enduring businesses in the past left no map, but they did show us the five crucial steps – to democratise, revolutionise, simplify, organise and author – that we need to take along the way.

Enduring leadership is not about starting up, selling up and putting your feet up. It's about leaving footprints in fresh sand, and staying on your feet through everything fortune throws at you. It's about facing those surprises with conviction and hunger, rather than a sigh. Waking up each day knowing that unforeseeable events, whether big or small, are going to challenge, educate and inspire you.

Leaders that endure know that there'll be unknown obstacles and opportunities on the journey – and that's where all the fun, as well as much of the frustration, is. If you are already sure you know what's going to happen, you can't have an adventure.

Acknowledgements

IN *Limitless* I share the stories of business wisdom that have inspired me. On this page I'd like to thank the people who made it possible: Peter Lyle, Susanna Abbott, Angela Ahrendts, Michael Andrew, Tesa Aragones, Matt Bain, Tom Bedecarré, Guy Bingley, Sir Richard Branson, Johnny Budden, Matty Corr, Raj Chaim, Dermott Cleary, Rhonda Crawford, Brendan DiBona, Trevor Edwards, Duan Evans, Louise Francis, James Hilton, Andy Hood, Jonathan Hum, Simon Jefferson, Richard John, Ben Jones, Sam Kelly, Romain Lartigue, Morwenna Loughman, Peter Lund, Francis MacGillivray, Diego Machado, Gino Mainolfi, Giles McCormack, Masaya Nakade, Geoff Northcott, Jean Oelwang, Joshua Ogden, Stefan Olander, Simon Pestridge, Jamie Oliver, Ron Peterson, Stéphanie Porter, Gail Rebuck, Erik Rogstad, Brian Skahan, Nicolai Smith, Sir Martin Sorrell, Scott Symonds, David Tait, Michael Tchao, Miles Unwin, Ian Wharton, Simon Willard, Hugo Veiga.